LIVING IN THE ZOO AND LOVING IT!

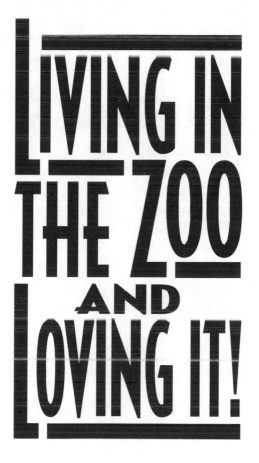

LIVING IN THE ZOO AND LOVING IT!

One Pastor's Life in the Ministry

GENE WILLIAMS

Beacon Hill Press of Kansas City
Kansas City, Missouri

ISBN 083-411-6014

Printed in the
United States of America

Cover design: Paul Franitza
Illustrations by Keith Alexander

Williams, Gene, 1932-
    Living in the zoo and loving it! / by Gene Williams.
        p.   cm.
    ISBN 0-8341-1601-4
    1. Williams, Gene, 1932-   2. Church of the Nazarene—Clergy—Biography. 3. Clergy—United States—Biography. I. Title.
    BX8699.N38W55   1995
    287.9'9'092—dc20
    [B]   95-31167
                                                                              CIP

10   9   8   7   6   5   4   3   2

To the wonderful laymen who,
for the past 45 years,
have with their love and support
enabled me to enjoy the incredible journey
of being their pastor.

And

To my wife, Joyce.
Without her love, encouragement, and support
this work would never have happened.

CONTENTS

Foreword   9

Introduction   11

1. **Arrested for an Awesome Adventure**   17

2. **A Funny Thing Happened on the Way to the Pulpit**   27

3. **Empty Pantries and Overdue Bills**   37

4. **Denying Delilah**   49

5. **Controlled Climates in Fiery Furnaces**   61

6. **You're Not a Very Good Daddy!**   75

7. **Friendly Keepers**   87

8. **Nobody's Perfect**   97

9. **Keeping Fresh in Dry Times**   107

10. **A Review of My Incredible Journey**   117

Notes   125

Foreword

It was at my urging that Gene Williams submitted this volume for publication. Once I started reading it, I could not put it down. I would subtitle it *How to Be a Pastor—and Love Every Minute of It!*

To know Gene Williams is to know that these pages flow out of his very life and ministry. Filled with realism and optimism, pathos and joy, vulnerability and unbounding confidence in the grace of God, this book touches on just about every area of struggle and triumph a pastor experiences.

Dr. Williams's phenomenal 25-year record as pastor of Wichita First Church of the Nazarene has earned him the right to pen these chapters. During his Wichita ministry he has received over 2,000 new members, two-thirds on profession of faith. He preaches to more than 1,400 each Sunday, twice the number when he became pastor in 1971, and for many years has conducted a widely viewed weekly television program. A middle-of-the-road Nazarene congregation, Wichita First gives $300,000 per year to the world mission program of the denomination and has built 27 buildings in world areas.

This, however, is not a book about Wichita First Church; it is a firsthand, engaging account of Dr. Williams's life and ministry, beginning with his call to preach and stories of his student pastorates, continuing through his maturing ministry. A listing of some of the chapters will give you an idea of what to expect in these pages:

A Funny Thing Happened on the Way to the
  Pulpit
Empty Pantries and Overdue Bills
Denying Delilah
Controlled Climates in Fiery Furnaces
You're Not a Very Good Daddy!
Keeping Fresh in Dry Times

But you must read these chapters, filled with anecdotes that will move you sometimes to laughter, sometimes to tears. All the while you will be reminded of the inestimable *privilege* of being a pastor of *human beings* with all their foibles and possibilities.

I highly recommend *Living in the Zoo and Loving It!* as one of the best books on practical theology I have ever read.

—William M. Greathouse
General Superintendent Emeritus
Church of the Nazarene

INTRODUCTION

Growing up as a young boy in Nashville, I was the runt of the neighborhood. When the gang got together to play ball, I was invariably one of the last ones chosen. It didn't matter if we were playing football, basketball, or baseball—I was just not big, strong, or fast enough to help win the game. Even in the eighth grade I was still playing on what Bailey Junior High School termed the "midget team."

Being chosen last should have warped my personality or affected me emotionally. It didn't—at least not from my perspective. Instead, it gave me a great appreciation for another "choosing of teams."

On the last Sunday night of May in 1949, Jesus said, "I chose you." I didn't have to move to the front of the gang and beg to be part of the team. Rather, He came looking for me and said, "I want you to be on my team."

At that time I didn't realize what a wonderful opportunity I was being given. I was just glad to make the team. Now I know that His choosing me to be on His team was one of the greatest honors and privileges I ever could have received. It is more magnificent than if I had been chosen for a Super Bowl or other championship team.

I have been through the "minor leagues," where I pastored some very small (how about 16 people?) churches. Then there were the larger churches of 250 to 400 people. And now I am privileged to pastor a very strong "major league" church.

Yes, there have been hardships and tough experiences all along the way. But there have also been some wonderful moments and rewards that have far exceeded my imagination. Mostly, though, there has been a deep inner satisfaction from being chosen by Jesus to be on His team. I am ecstatic about the opportunity He has given me.

We pastors sometimes refer to our environment as a "zoo." There is so much activity and so many different "creatures" that the word somehow seems fitting. While some of my colleagues struggle, I can honestly say that I am living in the "zoo"—and loving it!

The purpose of this book is to help those who are struggling to catch the joy of His will. Hopefully it will also encourage pastors who are enjoying their opportunity to relish this sacred privilege even more.

Life is not always easy in the ministry, but whomever God calls He enables and equips for each assignment. After choosing me, He—realizing I would need a lot of help—began to bring into my life people who would strengthen my efforts.

When I was a sophomore in college, God brought Bettye Murray into my life. This lovely lady and I shared five children and 39 years in the ministry. I am thankful He gave me someone to be a "teammate" in His kingdom as well as in my personal life. She was a great pastor's wife and mother to our children.

When Bettye was suddenly called to heaven, there was speculation as to what would happen to my career in the pastorate. But God had chosen me "to bear much fruit," as we read in John 15. In order to do that, I needed someone with whom to share this continued ministry. In His kindness and love, God brought Joyce McWhorter into my life. Our meeting was clearly arranged by God. With each passing day I thank Him more for this wonderful woman, who not only would not let me leave the "field of action" but also reenergized me. Without her loving support and encouragement, this book would never have been written. Thanks, Honey.

You will sense my pure joy at the privilege of being a pastor. Most of the laypersons I have been permitted to pastor have been much better to me than I deserve. I thank them for their love, prayers, and support.

Finally, I have been given five children who have responded in a wonderful way to their father's message. Thanks, kids.

One more time, let me thank my Heavenly Father for choosing the runt of the neighborhood to be on His team. What a wonderful privilege to play for the divine Coach!

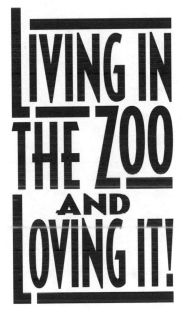

1
ARRESTED
FOR AN AWESOME ADVENTURE

My first inkling that something was wrong was the flashing red lights in my rearview mirror. I knew I had been driving safely—but a little strangely—as I had come around the courthouse square. The horn on my '41 Chevrolet coupe kept shorting out, and, in order to keep it from blowing, I had to make wide-sweeping turns. I had been preaching all day at a little country church in Hohenwald, Tennessee, and was headed home to Nashville. But there he was—blue uniform, gun, and badge—asking me if I had been drinking.

Imagine my chagrin when the officer said, "You're driving like a drunk man!" My friends in the car, who had come from Trevecca Nazarene College in Nashville to help me minister in this small church, were having the time of their lives laughing at my imminent arrest.

Snatches of newspaper headlines began to race through my mind as I envisioned them, such as

17

"Preacher Arrested for Drunk Driving on Courthouse Square." After the humiliating process of convincing the officer that I had spent the day preaching, not drinking, he said, "OK, Reverend. You've convinced me. I'm sorry for the inconvenience."

Imagine my relief. No ticket, no arrest—I was free to go on my way.

That was the second time I had felt the hand of authority laid on me. But the first time I *was* arrested—and I'm glad.

For you see, on the last Sunday night of May in 1949, I was apprehended by God. I had no idea what was in store—no concept of where the journey would lead—no vision of what the outcome would be. All I knew was that the divine hand of authority had been laid on me. I had been arrested for an awesome adventure—that of being a partner with God in building His kingdom.

Had I known then what I know now, I would have gladly volunteered to "do time" for the arresting Authority.

To me, being a God-called pastor is the most exciting option available.

I find it easy to identify with the joy Esther must have felt when God chose to work through her to bring freedom to the Jews who were under the penalty of death. Esther was also "arrested" by God, but this capture provided the greatest experience of her life—signing the decree that brought freedom to "all the Jews, young and old—women and little children" (Esther 3:13). What joy she must have experienced when King Xerxes gave her the signet ring to send out the decree of freedom to her people!

More than 40 years have passed since God gave me His signet ring with the authority to proclaim freedom to all who would listen and receive it. What an incredible assignment!

In spite of the awesome adventure offered to us, many pastors are discouraged, defeated, even despondent. Much is said about the pressure of the ministry, because there is pressure in pastoring. But then, what job *doesn't* have stress of some kind? I have four sons who work in various professional areas. Three are salesmen, and the other is a policeman. Talk about pressure—all four of them really work in pressure cookers: goals, quotas, reports, long work hours, customers to please, and bosses to be satisfied. These are the same types of pressures that seem to plunge so many pastors into distress.

I believe a great part of a pastor's problems originates in his or her mental attitude while approaching an assignment. Many have allowed the battle of their minds to exhaust them.

Chuck Swindoll, in his book *Living on the Ragged Edge*, speaks to a major source of pressure and makes three observations concerning an individual's inability to enjoy what he or she has:

1. The sensual lure of something better tomorrow robs us of the joys offered today.
2. The personal temptation to escape is always stronger than the realization of its consequences.

3. The final destination, if God is absent from the scene, will not satisfy.

He further observes, "The good life, the one that truly satisfies, exists only when we stop wanting a better one. It is the condition of savoring what is rather than longing for what might be." Finally, he states, "Satisfaction comes when we step off the escalator of desire and say, 'This is enough. What I have will do. What I make of it is up to me and my vital union with the living Lord.'"[1] Choosing to step off the escalator of desire in order to savor the incredible opportunity will go a long way toward keeping me focused on the great adventure rather than on the pressures along the way.

A positive mental attitude in any area of endeavor has a tremendous effect on the outcome. This is true of sports, business—in fact, in all arenas of life. But I am convinced that it is especially true of the ministry.

In his book *Man's Search for Meaning*, Viktor Frankl comments on why some people died in the death camps of World War II while others survived: "Man cannot control his circumstances, but he can control his attitude. This is the key to survival." He went on to say, "He who has a why to live can bear with almost any how."[2] Yes, pastors have some tough times, but their attitudes make all the difference in whether they are successes or failures.

Gary Collins points out in his book *The Magnificent Mind* the awesome power of the mind to work for us or against us. My mind works for me when I contemplate the pure joy of working with God.

I feel like John Donne, who is quoted by James Stewart in *Heralds of God* as having said in a message in London in 1620, "Who but myself can conceive of the sweetness of that salutation when the Spirit of God says to me in the morning, 'Go forth today and preach and preach consolation, preach peace, preach mercy.'"[3]

Samuel Chadwick is quoted in W. T. Purkiser's book *Image of the Ministry* as stating, "I would rather preach than eat my dinner or have a holiday. I would rather pay to preach than be paid not to preach. It has its place in the agony of sweat and tears. No calling has such joy and heartbreak, but it is a calling an archangel might covet, and I thank God that in His grace He called me into the ministry."[4]

So we're back to the basic issue. When the divine hand of God is laid on us—arresting us—what does that comprise? Is it an arrest for an adventure or a sentence to a concentration camp-like existence?

Oh, what a joy it is to agree with Stewart, who writes, "Every Sunday morning when it comes ought to find you awed and thrilled by the reflection. God is to be in action today through me for these people. This day may be crucial, this service decisive for someone now ripe for the vision of Jesus."[5]

The concept of adventure in the ministry doesn't stop in the pulpit.

It's also the awesome privilege of being at the point of need to be used by God to bring salvation, comfort, strength, hope, peace, and consolation. It's sharing the greatest news of the ages with a lost, hurting, and dying world.

We have heard many times about people who have experienced a rich sense of personal satisfaction and reward because they were at the point of need in someone's life. My son Brent is a policeman. He has received many citations of merit, which hang on his wall. These include one he received for saving an elderly man's life by administering cardiopulmonary resuscitation (CPR). Brent would be quick to say that he was just doing his job. But he would acknowledge that it was rewarding to realize that a life had been salvaged through his efforts. Randy, my son-in-law, is a physician in the emergency room of one of the great hospitals in Wichita. Occasionally one of his patients will come back to thank him for helping him. It is a very special time for him when that happens.

I can tell you that it is incredibly rewarding when those to whom I have ministered respond with statements like "You may not remember me, but you helped me find the Lord and get my life together." I have a very rewarding "warm fuzzy file" filled with such letters.

Some time ago I was preaching at a Sunday School convention in Ohio. A nice-looking young minister came to me and asked, "Do you remember preaching at the Ohio Youth Camp in 1967?"

"I sure do," I responded. "I'll never forget that wonderful week."

He then said, "That was the time when I settled the issues of my life, and now I pastor near here."

Truly, such testimonials are rewards for which I was arrested that May night more than 40 years ago.

I understand the need for pacing oneself so that burnout does not occur. No motor can run at full throttle constantly without blowing the engine. And we cannot keep up a continuously intense pace without blowing something. But our attitude will take us a long way toward coping with all facets of the ministry.

Recently my wife, Joyce, and I spent a couple of days at The Barn, a bed and breakfast inn near Valley Falls, Kansas. At breakfast we asked Tom Ryan, the proprietor, what he did to get away from the pressure. His response was interesting. He said, "When you love what you are doing, you don't have to get away." Tom is enjoying the adventure. And he doesn't consider it an incarceration to be "on duty" there every day.

Pastors must pace themselves and take time for family vacations. But the true adventure of pastoring begins with a healthy mental attitude.

In his beautiful book *God Works the Night Shift*, Ron Mehl presents some searching questions.

I guess it boils down to this: Do you want to be a part of what God is doing in our world, or do you choose to cut yourself off from that? Do you want to be an instrument ready for Him to pick up and use at a moment's notice, or do you want to collect dust like an old jar on some back shelf in a storeroom? Do you want to take part in a real spiritual contest with eternal implications, or do you want to sit on the bench and watch life slip by from the sidelines?[6]

I don't know about you, but I want to be a part of what God is doing in my world.

Several years ago while I was reading Matt. 16:18, in which Peter recognized the Lord's divinity, Jesus' response to Peter gripped me, for He said, "I *will* build my church" (emphasis added). As I read, I could almost hear Him whisper to me, "I will build my church—with you or without you." I want it to be *with* me. For you see, I am not much of a dust collector. In fact, I want to be out front—not in a storeroom out back.

I'd rather "participate" than "spectate" anytime. My heart would leap within me when my high school football coach would yell, "Get in there, Gene—we need you to make the next play work!" Believe me: I was never "all anything," but there was a place for me on the team, and I loved it.

My heart still leaps within me when the Master Coach says, "Gene, I need you to get this job done."

A few years ago while I was walking through our local Christian bookstore, The Better Book Room, looking for something to read, the title of Tim Hansel's book *Holy Sweat* virtually leaped off

the shelf. I believe it was because I had never con-
nected the words "holy" and "sweat." That concept
didn't quite match, so I knew I had to read the
book. It was worth reading to find two disconnect-
ed terms that united themselves together for me.
Hansel quotes Charlie Shedd, who said, "Lord, help
me to understand what you had in mind when you
made the original me."[7]

Hansel had written earlier, "Change your language. Don't say, 'I have to . . . ' because that auto-
matically produces resistance from within. Say instead, 'I choose to . . . '"[8]

I truly felt that God hooked those two thoughts
together in my mind in reverse order. We need to
pray that God will reveal what He had in mind
when He made the original "me." Then we must
change our language from "I have to . . ." to "I am
privileged to . . ."

**I understand that entering the ministry
must be the result of a divine call.
But our loving Father never
calls us to struggle through life.**

Jesus said in John 10:10, "I have come that they
[I] may have life, and have it to the full." So—the
call to preach is a call to a life of great joy.

When pastors move from the concept of "Woe
is me—I *have* to pastor" to "Thank God—I *get* to
pastor," then the joy of the awesome adventure becomes amazingly arresting.

2
A Funny Thing Happened on the Way to the Pulpit

A preacher without a sense of humor is in for some very uncomfortable experiences. We are working with some of God's funniest and most unpredictable creatures, so we might as well laugh. God made us as we are!

Surely you have heard the saying, "One of the best evidences that God has a sense of humor is the existence of man." If you have trouble with that, look around you at the people you meet. Honestly, some of us are really funny to look at. We come in all sizes, shapes, and colors.

I just love to watch people. It can be a riot just to sit back and observe people being themselves. I was sitting in the Denver airport on one of my trips and deliberately positioned myself where I could watch the "animals parading into their arks." It was hilarious. Some were fussing, others were off in "never-never land," and still others were visiting with friends and having fun. One thing was crystal clear—no two were alike. This must be how God felt as He watched Noah load the ark, I thought as I watched the passing parade.

It is this incredible variety of shapes and sizes of bodies, noses, ears, necks, and heads that gives us our different personalities. The next time you are tempted to think a giraffe is a funny-looking animal, spend some time in a major airport watching the people parade by. We are funny creatures—and there's nothing wrong with that!

Imagine how it would be if each one of us looked exactly alike—boring. So God designed a humorous variety of appearances that are often reflected in our actions.

It is this proneness to be human that causes some funny things to happen—even in church.

Anytime you get a group of God's funniest creatures together, be prepared for some things to happen that do not fit into the normal understanding of sacred activity.

Every person privileged by God to be a pastor needs to understand who he or she is working with. The pastor who comes to this point and does not learn to accept people where they are will live with the constant pressure of trying to put square pegs into round holes.

I'm not sure why we strain so much to turn a sacred opportunity for pleasure-filled worship into a solemn act that is, in too many cases, dull. I recognize the majesty and holiness of God. He is to be exalted, worshiped, and praised. But, remember: "It is he that hath made us, and not we ourselves" (Ps. 100:3, KJV). And He made us funny!

I have had some crazy experiences at not-so-crazy moments. If it were not for a God-given sense of humor, I would have surrendered my sanity long ago.

I'll never forget a Sunday afternoon baptismal service while I was pastoring in south Florida. I've never understood why some of our churches have not made better provision for this very special experience of baptism, but that's another story. On this beautiful Sunday afternoon we borrowed the facilities of a neighboring Baptist church. I was all set for the spiritual celebration that would climax with 15 new believers "following their Lord in baptism." You'll have to admit that this was a sanctimonious setting.

Well, it didn't quite work out that way. My pastor friend had forgotten to turn on the water heater, and the water was as cold as ice. Even in Florida the water comes out of the ground at about 72 degrees. Stepping into that without warning will get your attention in a hurry. No one realized the oversight until it was too late.

After the sacred preliminaries of songs, an appropriate message from God's Word, and a verbal affirmation from each candidate, we moved on to the solemn act of immersion. The moment I stepped into the pool, I realized something was wrong. I gasped as the cold water took my breath away. It was freezing! Now what could I do? I decided that I was the only one who would be standing in the water for any length of time and that I would just tough it out. It wasn't long before my legs were numb, and I couldn't really feel the cold.

As each person stepped into the water, we could hear the individual catch his or her breath. I saw expressions of near panic on those faces, but since I had them by the hand, I proceeded to baptize them as quickly as possible. It didn't take long for everyone present to catch on to what had happened, but none of us anticipated what was coming.

Without my knowledge, a young girl of about 15 years of age joined the line of candidates. We had worked hard over the years to make her feel loved and accepted, so I would not embarrass her now by declining to baptize her. But I was not, I repeat, *not* prepared for what happened next.

This young lady had watched 10 people endure the icy water as they were baptized before she stepped into the pool. Notice that key word *stepped*—for, you see, she then decided on a different approach. She called out, "Cold water never bothered me!" and with that dove head first into the pool. Water went everywhere.

I caught her as she swam by me, guiding her into a quick U-turn and back up the steps. To this day I'm not sure if she was truly baptized or not. The words I said were *not* "I baptize you in the name of the Father, Son, and Holy Spirit."

Any resemblance of solemnity was gone from that service. The congregation and I laughed out loud (in *church*), and then we proceeded with the service. It was hilarious.

Such hilarity could wreck a guy's "preacheri-ness" if he allowed that to happen. I'm grateful that God has enabled me to learn to laugh at things I cannot help. I try to learn from the situation, although sometimes I just can't seem to keep up.

After that experience in the cold water of south Florida, I always check the temperature in the pool just before the service. In my present church I did that one evening and found it to be nice and warm. I promptly went to the furnace room to turn off the valve so the water would not get too hot. I then returned to my study to make my final mental preparations for the evening service.

At the proper time the beaming new Christians came forward to participate in this beautiful moment. They gave public affirmation of their faith, and it was a touching time for all of us. Then they went on their way to prepare for baptism, and I went my way so we could meet at the pool.

Only then, at the baptistery, did we realize that there was no water in the pool. Can you imagine my chagrin when it became obvious that I had turned the wrong valve? The pool had drained dry while we were singing and having a great service.

At a time like that one will either laugh or cry. I chose to laugh. I confessed my ineptness as a plumber while my face turned several hues of bright red. The congregation laughed with me, and we all went home planning to attend another "sacred service" at a later time.

One never knows when something will go wrong. There is no more solemn occasion than a funeral or burial service—yet even then we must be ready for some odd occurrences. I remember one bitterly cold January day driving in a funeral procession to a small country cemetery. When we arrived at the burial site, we knew immediately that something was wrong. There was no tent to protect the funeral party from the cold wind. Not only was there no tent, but there was no rack upon which to place the casket at the gravesite. There was just an ominous hole in the hard, frozen, snow-packed ground.

The mortician and I sized up the situation and proceeded with the quickest committal in history. What else do you do when the chill factor is −42 degrees? It wasn't funny, but neither was it the tragedy it could have been had either of us let the situation dictate our attitudes. We did what we needed to do and added another experience to our scrapbook of memories.

Speaking of funerals, nothing I have ever experienced compares with what happened at a service where my friend, Eugene Simpson, was officiating. In one of his pastorates there was a family with four sets of twins, all girls. Two sets of these twins seemed more like a set of quadruplets, because there was only a year's difference in their ages, and all four were often dressed alike.

When these four girls were 20 and 21 years of age, one of them got married. About a year later the couple had a baby. Unfortunately, the infant lived only a few days. As their pastor, Gene had the funeral for this newborn baby, a very sad occasion. As they were leaving the funeral home after the service, the young mother fainted in the foyer. The attendants laid her out on the floor. Within a minute or so, the other three sisters also fainted and were laid out on the floor side by side. After a few hectic moments, they were revived enough to proceed to the funeral car and make their way to the cemetery for the committal.

Following the brief service, the young mother took three or four steps and fainted again. Bystanders laid her on the grassy hillside. Again, one by one, the other three sisters also passed out and were laid next to their sister.

Now what does a pastor do in a situation like that? No, it isn't funny, and yet it is. A minister learns to make the most of every situation, and sometimes that means laughter. It is very difficult to make every experience in church a sacred one. And Gene could hardly tell me his story for laughing. Maybe that's why he, too, has remained in God's ministry more than 40 years.

I could tell you of times I have made some major blunders while preaching, and my face has beamed like a Christmas tree. There were times when babies spit up on me (or worse) during dedication services. There were weddings like that of my sister, Joyce Ann, in which the candles ignited the ferns. Since I had my back to the candles, I was the last one to realize what was happening.

There have been other equally hilarious things

that have happened at weddings. On one very formal occasion I was really into the solemnity of the service until I invited a very nervous groom to "put this fing on her ringer." The last syllable was hardly out of my mouth before the entire wedding party doubled up in unholy mirth.

Now, I had a choice. I could have taken the position that I was incapable of doing weddings or that they were just a job to perform. However, I have learned to relax. If something goes wrong, it's not the end of the world. As a result, I have presided over the fainting of brides and quaking of grooms and in the process gathered some very pleasant memories.

Oh, sure—there have been some weird and uncomfortable encounters with brides who thought the world was supposed to stop for their wedding. And there have been a smattering of parents who ordered everyone around, thereby making us all uncomfortable. But the good times, fun times, and happy memories are so many that I frankly look forward to every opportunity to share in this most special moment in a young couple's life.

Also I have experienced interruptions in church services at the most inopportune moments. I was a 19-year-old, "gourd green" pastor at the small church in Hohenwald, Tennessee (mentioned earlier), when, in my first service there, I received quite an indoctrination into "unexpected experiences."

I was doing my best to lead this tiny congregation in the worship service. Having been raised in the wonderful atmosphere of First Church of the Nazarene in Nashville, I had a good idea of how a service should proceed, or so I thought. After the hymns, offering, and pastoral prayer, it was time for the message of the morning. Then I got the shock of my young life. Just as I finished reading the scripture text for the morning, a young mother on the second row to my left decided it was time to nurse her baby! That was a new sight to my young eyes. It was such a natural thing for her to do that she didn't even use a diaper or blanket to cover up the "distraction." I learned very quickly the fine art of tunnel vision. God helped me to focus my eyes on a little old grandmother on the back row to my right. As I said earlier, I had never seen such a sight—and this was no time to start looking!

That was the first of many interruptions over the years. Looking back on that first day in the pulpit as a pastor, I believe my Heavenly Father was preparing me for many more to come.

Years later when I was pastoring in Princeton, Florida, I had an experience that could have wrecked the service. I had a special message for my people and felt the burden of the hour. I was coming to a major point in this serious message. After making a profound statement and pausing to let it sink in, a little old man spoke up and said in a voice heard by all, "What I want to know is what are you going to do about those Japanese bombers on the Burma road?"

It was a totally off-the-wall interruption that caught everyone by surprise. The congregation just sat there bouncing in their pews, choking back their laughter. I responded in one word, "Nothing," and then proceeded with the message. Amazingly, God helped us to complete a good service.

The people knew that the little man had emotional problems as a result of being in the armed services during World War II. Sure, there was a snicker or two, but the people really appreciated the fact that we didn't let an "odd, unplanned encounter" take charge of the service.

I guess one of the best ways to summarize what I am trying to convey is "Lighten up."

Learn to be flexible.

We know that great bridges move several feet as they flex with the load of the moment. I currently pastor several engineers of the Boeing Aircraft Company. They assure me that if there is no flexibility in the wings of the great airplanes they make, the craft would surely break with the strain of unexpected turbulence. Perhaps we preachers need to learn that our survival in the great calling God has given us is greatly enhanced if we learn to yield to the unexpected things that are going to occur.

Funny—even weird—things are going to happen, and laughing is a lot better than choking on one's dignity!

3
Empty Pantries and Overdue Bills

"Honey, I'm coming home for lunch. I'll be there in just a few minutes."

Bettye shocked me with her response: "There's no need to come home. We have no food in the house." Then she asked, "Do you have any money?"

"No, but it's lunchtime, and I'm coming home anyway."

It was 1958, and I was pastoring a home mission church in Gainesville, Florida. When I arrived home, imagine my surprise when I discovered she wasn't kidding—there really *wasn't* a single morsel of food in the house. We had no money, and this was in precredit card days. So how do you feed three hungry children and two adults with absolutely nothing?

I gathered three cartons of pop bottles from the garage and under the house and returned them to the grocery store for the 45-cent deposit. That was enough to buy a can of tomato soup, a tube of crackers, and a package of Kool-Aid. I was relieved to have something for the kids to eat. How do you tell three small children, "It's prayer and fasting day—think of the joy of having nothing to eat and getting to pray for those who are less fortunate than we are"?

It just didn't make sense. Bettye and I as adults could forego food for the pleasure of prayer and fasting, but we were grateful for the soup and crackers for the children. After we sat down I thanked God for the meal, and the kids began to eat.

While we were eating, the telephone rang. Mrs. Adams, one of the 12 members of that little church, was calling to ask, "Mrs. Williams, what's wrong at the parsonage?"

Bettye replied, "Nothing. There's nothing wrong."

"Yes, there *is* something wrong," Mrs. Adams responded. "When I was having my devotions this morning, God laid your little family on my heart."

Bettye said, "If you had called earlier, I would have told you we had nothing to eat."

She then shared with Mrs. Adams what I had done. We did, indeed, have food for lunch. Bettye also told her that this was payday, and I would get my weekly check in the amount of $50.00 at prayer meeting that evening. We would be fine—she was not to worry about us.

I don't know how many phone calls Mrs. Adams made that afternoon, but before suppertime that evening she and her son-in-law backed a station wagon loaded with food to the front door of that little parsonage. We had a full storehouse of food. They even cooked the chicken! That's the closest we ever came to missing a meal. But I do have to say that God never forsook us. We never had to beg for bread. We always felt a sense of security for the material needs of our lives.

One of the most common pressure points with which all pastors wrestle is how they will survive financially or materially in this world.

Too often we hear the war stories of those who could not make ends meet. This is very clearly a major pressure point in the ministry. The lack of adequate support has, according to a survey conducted by *Leadership* magazine, created financial problems that require 69 percent of the spouses of pastors to work outside the home. Money struggles are listed by H. B. London Jr. and Neil Wiseman in *Pastors at Risk* as a major reason the pastoral ministry is so difficult today.[1]

The financial support scale for many pastors is far less than it ought to be. However, David wrote, "I have never seen the righteous forsaken or their children begging bread" (Ps. 37:25). Somehow, someway, God provides for all His people.

Jesus said,

> For this reason I say to you, do not be anxious for your life, as to what you shall eat, or what you shall drink; nor for your body, as to what you shall

put on. Is not life more than food, and the body than clothing? Look at the birds of the air, that they do not sow, neither do they reap, nor gather into barns, and yet your heavenly Father feeds them. Are you not worth much more than they? And which of you by being anxious can add a single cubit to his life's span? And why are you anxious about clothing? Observe how the lilies of the field grow; they do not toil nor do they spin, yet I say to you that even Solomon in all his glory did not clothe himself like one of these. But if God so arrays the grass of the field, which is alive today and tomorrow is thrown into the furnace, will He not much more do so for you, O men of little faith? Do not be anxious then, saying, "What shall we eat?" or "What shall we drink?" or "With what shall we clothe ourselves?" *(Matt. 6:25-31, NASB).*

Are those words for laypersons only? I think not. Do they not also apply to the man behind the pulpit? I think so. If I understand anything at all that Jesus is saying, He is clearly committing the Father to take care of those who trust Him. Maybe the key phrase in all of that is in the last verse (v. 31): "Do not be anxious." As those who are God-called for the special assignment of pastoring God's people, we are to become people of faith in God's promises. That faith eliminates anxiety. Anxiety is worry without hope, and we are not without hope. We may not always understand how He will take care of us, but we know He will provide for those He calls to special assignments.

It would be easy for someone to say to me, "That's easy for *you* to say. You pastor a large church and are well cared for." That's true. I'm much better paid than I ever dreamed I would be. However, there have been some tough times along the way. I learned early that God does not abandon those who have absolute faith in Him.

In 1956 Bettye and I left Nashville for seminary in Kansas City in a '41 Chevrolet coupe that had 100,000 miles on it. I had $50.00 in my pocket, no job awaiting me in Kansas City, and a six-week-old baby. In retrospect, it seems a reckless thing to do. At the moment it seemed the *only* thing to do in response to God's call to preach His Word and my need to be prepared. There's something about "naive faith" that's beautiful, and God seems to find that irresistible. We were obviously naive in leaving Nashville for Kansas City. God must have called a whole platoon of angels to be on standby to watch over two inexperienced kids of faith.

We moved in with some friends until I could find work. Before the week was over I had a job in hand, and we were able to get our own apartment— if you could call one room and a back porch with a shared bath an apartment. Finally, I could begin to carry out what I knew God wanted me to do. I was ready to settle in and prepare for God's calling on my life. That call had become my life's focus.

There were many scary times when there just wasn't enough money. Still, we never missed a meal, and we had enough clothes to wear. God seemed always to know just what we were going to need.

During my second year in seminary, a second child came to bless our home. This put an even heavier financial burden on us. Help from family members was totally out of the question, but help from God is always a reality. While carrying a full-time load at the seminary and working 40 hours a week in a grocery store, I was given the opportunity to pastor a little country church 65 miles from our home in Kansas City. Early on Sunday mornings we drove to Mirabile, Missouri, ministered to the people the best we could, spent the afternoon in someone's home, and drove back to Kansas City late Sunday night. Whatever was given in the offering was my salary. Sometimes it helped, but many times I barely broke even with gas expenses.

Pastoring that little country church wasn't too difficult during the summertime, although I'll confess there were times when my 100 percent wool suit (my only suit) was wringing wet with sweat as a result of preaching in that small building that sat under the boiling sun and had no air conditioning. However, when winter came, the journey became a tougher challenge. I especially recall those Sundays when it snowed and was bitter cold.

It was on one of those frigid days that God inspired a good layman to give me his topcoat that happened to be made of heavy mohair. Never mind that it was a hand-me-down. It was warm, and before the night was over it would come in very handy—for on the way home late that night, something went wrong with the motor of the car, and we were stranded on the side of a cold winter highway. Because of God's provision, I had a coat to break the wind and keep me warm until I could get help with the car.

I wouldn't take anything for the experiences of those early years at seminary. It was there I learned that the same God who feeds the birds and clothes the lilies of the field also feeds His own and clothes them too. I also learned the rich rewards of those experiences at that little country church.

While I was pastoring there, a young father went out to hunt rabbits. When he did not return at dark, his wife called her father, who went looking and found the body of this young husband and father—the victim of a tragic hunting accident. On a recent trip back to Mirabile, I visited an old country store, where a group of farmers was sitting around a potbellied stove on a rainy day. One of those farmers was the son of that man. He was 10 days old when he lost his dad. What joy and satisfaction it was to visit with him and talk about his dad!

I also stopped at the home of one of the church couples, who are now in their 80s. They were so happy to see me, and we rejoiced together as we shared memories of hot summer days and cold winter nights of nearly 40 years ago.

The memories of that visit reminded me again of the tender, loving care of a Father who thinks more of His highest creatures than He does of sparrows and lilies. It was also richly rewarding to know that I had been a vital part of their lives.

There have been many other times when, if it had not been for divine provision, I would have found myself in real financial trouble.

It's no secret that traveling with four young children is quite a challenge. That trial is greatly magnified if one of the children happens to become ill. On one of our vacation journeys from Princeton, Florida, to Nashville, Brent became very critically ill. Initially we thought his fever was merely from a cold or a mild case of the flu. But by the time we had traveled the six hours to the Florida-Georgia state line, it became obvious that this was no minor problem. His fever was so high that it felt like it could burn our hands when we touched him.

Upon inquiry we found that the closest major hospital was in Valdosta, Georgia, so we headed there as fast as we could safely travel. It didn't take the physician long to determine that our precious two-year-old was seriously ill with bronchial pneumonia. They placed him in an oxygen tent and on an ice mattress. Bettye stayed at the hospital with Brent while I checked into a motel with the other kids.

Two extra days in a motel and an unexpected hospital stay did not fit into our travel budget. So I called back to Princeton and spoke to a friend about a loan to help us pay these unanticipated bills.

He did more than make the loan. He called some of our members who were vacationing in southern Georgia and informed them of the problems our family was having. Imagine our surprise when they showed up that morning to visit the parsonage family at the hospital. Since it was Sunday, the three healthy kids and I worshiped with them at the Valdosta Church of the Nazarene.

Upon returning to the hospital, we knew Brent was better. While Bettye was napping, he had pulled the plug on the ice mattress. She had been awakened by a pool of water flooding the floor.

After mopping the floor, the weary nurse checked with the attending physician, who decided it was safe to allow us to continue our journey. Imagine the joy I felt in my heart when I went to the business office to make arrangements for payment for Brent's care and was informed nothing was due. Our dear friends from home had paid the bill in full.

I could go on and on with story after story of how God has provided for us in times of crisis. For the first 25 years of my ministry, there were no savings accounts, no tax-sheltered annuities. It was truly hand-to-mouth, or payday to payday. But we lived—we made it. The experience in Gainesville, Florida, described earlier, was the closest we ever came to hunger. There was rarely a surplus, never a savings account, but neither did we ever go without the absolute necessities of life.

> **There is no way to convey the peace that comes with having a naive trust in God's promises.**

I understand that there are those who don't have much of this world's goods. However, I will have to say that at times I sometimes am afraid we expect to have too much of this world's goods. Some young couples get married and expect to have in the first few years of their marriage what it took their parents many years to acquire. It seems to me that some young pastors expect early in their ministry to reap the benefits that it has taken others of us 25 or more years to acquire.

Are we trying to get too far too fast? Have we lost the sense of naive faith that sparrows have and that has sustained the rest of God's creation? They take the provisions of God without questioning or complaining. Maybe we need to work hard, trust completely, and then we will see what God can do.

From those early years I truly understand being underpaid and having poor financial support. But maybe—just maybe—we have given Satan a hammer to use in driving us into the ground when the God who multiplies fish and bread wants to demonstrate His providential care.

We may need to be bivocational. In fact, that was my experience when pastoring that small church in Gainesville. Following our empty pantry experience, I looked for some way to augment my $50.00-per-week salary. I was able to supplement my income by teaching school. This opened many opportunities in the community. If a bivocational stint becomes necessary, teaching is a natural avenue. In some cases it may be necessary for the spouse to work outside the home. But I hope this is only from necessity, not for luxury.

We do not need to permit this pressure to rob us of the joy and peace that rightfully belongs to all of God's people. And I believe these fruits belong especially to faithful pastors.

The pantry may be empty and the bills overdue, but we will make it because He never forsakes those who have absolute faith in Him and His provision. After all, Peter did walk on water. The water was turned into wine. Lazarus did come forth.

There was bread and fish for everyone. The nets were full.

I really believe God still has trouble resisting naive faith. Hence, it is easy for me to echo the testimony of David in Ps. 37:25, "I have never seen the righteous forsaken or their children begging bread." And I do not believe He would start a new program by forsaking me now!

4
DENYING DELILAH

I was young and energetic and desperately wanted to be a good pastor. So when the call came, my first instinct was to respond to the request immediately. The voice on the phone sounded pitiful. However, something said, "Think. Be careful." And I am truly glad for that inner voice. It may very well have saved everything that I hold precious.

It was the height of the Vietnam War, and many of our young men were serving there. They had left their wives and children in a variety of living arrangements around Homestead Air Base near Homestead, Florida. I was pastoring the Princeton Church of the Nazarene, located about three miles from the main entrance of the base. We were doing our best to minister to many of these young families.

It was about 10 P.M. on a Saturday night when I received this call. The distraught young lady was one of those wives who was living there with her two small children. The conversation went something like this:

"Pastor, this is . . ." And she told me her name. "I need to talk with you."

I responded, "OK, I'll be glad to help you. I'll see you at church tomorrow, and we can set a time to get together."

"Pastor, I really need to talk to you tonight," she insisted.

"It's late—is this an emergency?" I asked. "Have you heard from your husband? Is he all right?"

"I realize it's late. I haven't heard from my husband. It's me I'm calling about. I'm tired of living this way, and life isn't worth the effort. I can't go on. I'm going to do something tonight," she threatened.

This alarmed me. The fear that something tragic could indeed happen was frightening. My pastoral instincts were to respond quickly.

The conversation continued as I asked her, "Can you come to the parsonage? Bettye and I will be happy to visit and pray with you."

She answered, "No, I can't leave the trailer. My kids are asleep, and I have no one to watch them. Please come. I must talk with you tonight."

Her voice sounded so desperate that I agreed to go. I would get there as quickly as possible.

It was at this point I heard the voice that I am confident is God's guidance system through the mine fields of life. "Don't go alone," the voice said. "Take someone with you."

My wife couldn't go, because our four small children were asleep. So I called a friend, Ray Oney, who was on the church board, and asked if he could make a call with me. He said he would be glad to go with me. I picked him up, and we drove to the Isle of Gold Trailer Park on U.S. Highway 1.

Am I ever glad for that inner voice! As Ray and I walked quietly, prayerfully toward the trailer to help a lady in distress, we received the shock of our lives. We could hear soft music and noticed that the lights had been turned down low. I knocked on the trailer door as my friend Ray stood in the shadows behind me. When the young wife came to the door, she was dressed in a very revealing nightgown.

I am still amazed at the "healing" power of my words: "Ray and I are here to help you."

Suddenly she was fine and no longer needed to talk. "Thank you for coming, Pastor, but I'm fine now," she said. "I'll be OK. Sorry for disturbing you."

I am absolutely convinced that had I not brought my friend along with me, I could have been ruined for life. It wasn't counseling she wanted. Although I would have resisted the temptation to be physically involved with her, her accusations could have tarnished me for life.

Why share this? Because every minister will have a "Delilah" in his or her life. Some of these might come as a temptation to perform an immoral act. Another might be the temptation to unwisely use the power that accompanies being the chosen leader of a group of people. Another source of temptation might be to pursue financial rewards that are made available. Still another temptation might be the heady feeling that can follow the adulation that may come with being a public figure.

Whatever form she takes, Delilah must be denied. Wise is the minister who avoids these temptations to turn aside from the pursuit of his or her calling to be a good shepherd to the flock God has entrusted to him or her.

Delilah will probably come in one of these forms: passion, pride, or possessions. Let's look at them individually.

The Delilah Named Passion

Since I began this chapter with a true story from my own life, let's look at this "Delilah" first. Jack Wilson authored *But Thou, O Man of God*, an excellent book on the pastoral ministry. In it he aptly points out, "There is never a waiver on the Sixth Commandment."[1] This is true for all of us. We ministers have no leeway in the keeping of the commandments. There are no, I repeat, *no* justifiable circumstances.

We must understand that, for some reason, being in the public eye in a position of high visibility has a way of making a person, any person, sexually attractive to some people. This is true of entertainers, athletes, politicians, and ministers.

The minister who refuses to disgrace his or her calling must learn to recognize the danger signs. The minister must not lose sight of his or her position as the spiritual leader of the flock.

The temptation to be intimately involved most often occurs during counseling settings, when the communication of understanding, sympathy, and tenderness seems to draw the counselee to the pastor. This situation becomes explosive when the minister is unhappy with the sexual response of his or her own spouse.

A lady is complaining that her husband is not paying enough attention to her and explains how alone she feels. The pastor begins to think about how his wife is not responding to him and reflects how alone *he* feels. He thinks, "If only my wife were like her." She thinks, "If only my husband were like him." From this encounter to a warm holding of hands "in prayer," then later a kindly hug at the end of the session—and Delilah is on her way to destroying the ministry of God's man.

A second area where this Delilah plays havoc is in those with whom we work closely. A very good pastor friend of mine carried on a two-year affair with his secretary *in his study* at the church. When I confronted him, he said, "We always had prayer after we had sex and asked God for forgiveness."

That is the most presumptuous and ridiculous response imaginable. There is no justification for immorality, and this is particularly true for the person who would be a spiritual leader.

Run from this Delilah! Do not let her rob you of the power of God in your life. There may be forgiveness and perhaps restoration, but know this: the cloud of that sin will never go away. Jack Wilson, quoted previously, goes on to write, "Repercussions for our sins cannot be retracted with forgiveness."[2] I believe he's right.

Solomon wrote in Prov. 6:27-35:

> Can a man scoop fire into his lap without his clothes being burned? Can a man walk on hot coals without his feet being scorched? So is he who sleeps with another man's wife; no one who touches her will go unpunished. Men do not despise a thief if he steals to satisfy his hunger when he is starving. Yet if he is caught, he must pay sevenfold, though it costs him all the wealth of his house. But a man who commits adultery lacks judgment; whoever does so destroys himself. Blows and disgrace are his lot, and his shame will never be wiped away; for jealousy arouses a husband's fury, and he will show no mercy when he takes revenge. He will not accept any compensation; he will refuse the bribe, however great it is.

Hear ye! Hear ye!

The Delilah Named Pride

Many of us who are able to resist the temptation to sins of passion fall prey to the sin of pride.

The fact that we are adulated and exercise a certain amount of power over the lives of those in our congregations can cause us to swell with the pride of the Pharisee who opposed Jesus, unless we stay on guard against it.

Remember: Satan does not care *how* he ruins our ministry—as long as he *does*. He will stop at nothing to disqualify us, and a pastor full of pride with the accompanying harshness, aloofness, and dictatorial spirit will be disqualified as a spiritual leader.

Pastors are shepherds, and shepherds are the very epitome of kindness and gentleness. They are the opposite of pride. In his book *A Minister's Obstacles*, Ralph Turnbull writes, "No man can bear witness to Christ and to himself at the same time. No man can give the impression that he himself is clever and that Christ is mighty to save."[3] He goes on to write, "A Christian worker lives in the glare of publicity which may well dazzle him. Here he is met with the adulation of the world, the foolish, and the well-meaning who each in their turn bring their contribution to feed the fire of self-admiration and esteem. It is right that we see ourselves in relation to this peril."[4]

Indeed, we will either see ourselves in relation to this peril or be destroyed by it. But how do we resist this temptation?

One way is to remember that in and of ourselves we are nothing.

It is not our cleverness that people admire. It is the power of God working in us.

We do well to remember that whatever we are to be, we are to be like Jesus. He was a servant, and he who would be like Jesus must have a servant's heart.

Years ago, a ministerial friend of mine said he did not believe a minister could drink coffee and chit-chat with his parishioners during the week and then be elevated to his proper status on Sunday morning. You will not be surprised to learn he has long since left the pastoral ministry.

Jesus said, "Whoever wants to be first must be your slave—just as the Son of Man did not come to be served, but to serve" (Matt. 20:27-28).

Every time I'm tempted to think of myself in a prideful way, I review the account of Jesus as He washed the disciples' feet. If the Master was willing to be a servant, who am I to lord my position over anyone?

Then, too, there is great joy and satisfaction in being a good servant to appreciative people. On Labor Day 1972 I began a special experience of love with my congregation. I had moved to Wichita, Kansas, from Homestead, Florida. While in Homestead I had learned to cook fish for large crowds of people. So I suggested we have a church fish fry on Labor Day.

Every year since then, we've had a Labor Day fish fry. I have prepared and cooked more than three tons of catfish. Work? You bet! But fun? Absolutely! Would I start it all over again if I were free of the obligation? In a minute!

You see, my people love it. They come to the cooker and tease about how they like to see me sweat. And believe me, I *do* sweat when it's 100 degrees in Kansas!

This is not a sophisticated thing to do, but the people have responded in a warm and wonderful way. And I love doing something for my people. This kind of activity helps keep me from the temptation of a Delilah named Pride.

The Delilah Named Possessions

Don't be surprised when the lovely, attractive seductress named Possessions pays her call. After all, most ministers live just above the poverty line and have very little security laid up for retirement years.

In their searching book *Pastors at Risk*, H. B. London Jr. and Neil Wiseman make a clear statement concerning pastors' financial situations: "The clearer the call the fewer the complaints; and income is less frequently the measure of ministry. For those pastors whose sense of vocation is not so sharp, finances become a measure of personal worth and affect self-esteem."[5]

I want to emphasize the phrase "The clearer the call the fewer the complaints." We will be tempted to feel sorry for ourselves unless we remember: "Foxes have holes and birds of the air have nests, but the Son of Man has no place to lay his head" (Luke 9:58).

We have already discussed "empty pantries and unpaid bills" and the fact that God meets our needs as well. But what of the other end of the spectrum?

Some pastors are subjected to opportunities for strong financial gain. Usually, the stronger the congregation the more one will need to be alert to the temptation to become involved in business opportunities. I know some good persons, great preachers, who could resist the temptation of moral failure. And they understood their need for God, so pride made no inroads. Their failure came when they ventured into the business world and were successful.

Maybe I am too conservative, but I believe a minister's greatest business opportunity is God's business. To be at our best in His business, we need to keep both eyes on "the prize of the high calling of God in Christ Jesus" (Phil. 3:14, KJV).

Let it be clearly understood that the qualities that make one successful in the ministry closely parallel those necessary to make one successful in the secular world. So it is easy to see why some ministers prosper in business ventures.

Pastoring a church is a full-time job and deserves our undivided attention. I understand that some pastors have to work because they do not earn a living wage. However, in my opinion, those who can live on the support provided by their church should do so.

It's very difficult to keep your mind uncluttered and sensitive to the voice of God at the time you're faced with a major business decision. Many years ago I was driving home from hospital calling, and as I rode along I was thinking of a business decision. At that time I had not resisted this temptation. In fact, I justified my involvement with the realization that I could have three kids in college at the same time, and the financial needs would be enormous.

As I drove along U.S. Highway 1, I was considering the business decision when God interrupted my thoughts: "And what are you preaching to your people this Sunday?" It was Tuesday, and I had not started any preparation.

I understood the message, went to my business partner, and got out of the business deal immediately. I promised God that I would live on the level provided by the support of my church and would stay free from any encumbrances that would use mental energy that needed to be devoted to the Kingdom.

Since then I have not violated that trust, and God has blessed my life beyond my wildest dreams. I never thought I would enjoy the material blessings I have. And what about the children I worried about educating? Four of the five children who call me "Dad" have college degrees. The other, my only daughter, opted for marriage.

**Resist the temptation to split your
love, interest, time, and energy
for the benefit of material gain.
You will never regret it.**

Deny Delilah! She comes in many, many shapes and under numerous names. Satan will do everything he can to defeat you. Just remember: "No temptation has seized you except what is common to man. And God is faithful; he will not let you be tempted beyond what you can bear. But when you are tempted, he will also provide a way out so that you can stand up under it" (1 Cor. 10:13).

5

CONTROLLED CLIMATES IN FIERY FURNACES

As I listened to him across the breakfast table in that little family restaurant, I could hardly believe my ears. This man should have been my closest ally. He should have been the lay leader of the church. After all, he was our Sunday School superintendent and a prominent attorney in the community. In addition to this, he had grown up in that church with his large extended family. He should have been used of God in a wonderful way. Surely I didn't hear him say what I thought he said.

But I did. He said it. As coolly and calmly as you can imagine, this layman looked directly at me and said, "Pastor, I really think you should leave. You're much too young to be pastoring this church, and it would be best for everyone if you'd resign. I know you have a vote coming up. You'd be smart not to put the church through the trauma of a bad vote."

I should have been stunned, but I wasn't. I simply didn't believe him. One of us was misreading this situation, and I believed it to be him. Perhaps I was naive. But being naive sometimes gives one great protective covering. There was no question that God had brought me to this church, and I took confidence in that wonderful certainty. The people were responding to my leadership, and I was building the ministry of that congregation in the absolute confidence that I was where God wanted me to be. I had not sought the call to pastor that church. In fact, I was selected to be pastor before I even knew I was being considered.

I know there are times when a pastor needs to move on (I *think*), although I believe short-term pastorates are a curse of the church. I will concede, however, that sometimes a pastor's personality does not align itself with the personality of the church, and in those cases he or she needs to move. To remain stubbornly in such situations is not right and is an injustice to the Kingdom.

However, I must reiterate that the situation in my case did not involve a misfit. I had been there as pastor for two years, the church was growing, and I honestly believed the people loved me.

What was this man's problem?

I discovered that he was involved in some political maneuvering on that district. When he didn't get the support from his local church on "his side" of the issue, someone had to feel his wrath. Guess who that was? You're right—it was me! And that's OK.

There's something about a naive faith that seems to place one in God's protective custody mentally, emotionally, spiritually, and even sometimes physically. I was catching the heat at full strength, but, as I would learn, God was still totally in charge. I proceeded to take the pastoral vote, and the results were wonderful. There were 94 favorable and only 4 negative votes. Surely now he would see his mistake and join the team. Wrong. I kept meeting with this man to try to minister to him and bring him onto the team at the church. But the hostile atmosphere intensified with each succeeding meeting.

His explanation of the vote only heated up the furnace hotter than ever. I'll never forget his words: "Don't take comfort in the vote. A lot of people never have voted against a pastor, and they just didn't want to start now." He went on to say, "I didn't vote against you, but I sure didn't vote *for* you either."

So the furnace got hotter and hotter. How does one survive such a blistering experience?

I believe the Hebrews of Dan. 3:16-18 give us great insight and inspiration. These three young men knew who they were, and they had an irrefutable commitment to God. They were committed to a life of absolute trust in Jehovah. Theirs was a naive faith. They did not have to know "how" things would work. They just knew that they belonged to God. They would leave the results of their faith to Him. Listen to their response to the king: "O Nebuchadnezzar, we do not need to defend ourselves before you in this matter. If we are thrown into the blazing furnace, the God we serve is able to save us from it, and He will rescue us from your hand, O king. But even if he does not, we want you to know, O king, that we will not serve your gods or worship the image of gold you have set up" (Dan. 3:16-18).

God cannot resist faith like that. And even though the enemy makes the furnace "seven times hotter than usual," he cannot make the furnace hot enough to penetrate God's protective presence.

The hotter the furnace, the closer He wraps himself around us. He insulates us from the heat of the predicament.

How does a pastor develop this faith? He or she understands that what we promise to others also works for us. For example, the promise of a "Wonderful Counselor, Mighty God, Everlasting Father, Prince of Peace" in Isa. 9:6 is not just for laypersons.

It is not unusual for a pastor to feel the pressure that comes from determining the direction of his or her ministry. I remind you that every minister of the gospel is eligible for the confidence provided in Prov. 3:5-6: "Trust in the LORD with all your heart and lean not on your own understanding; in all your ways acknowledge him, and he will make your paths straight."

God in His kindness taught me early simply to trust His guidance. In my very first pastorate, at the ripe old age of 19, I learned to trust Him to lead me through the mine fields of pastoral relationships.

Hohenwald, Tennessee, where I was pastoring, was a small, rural, hill country town, and the church exemplified the character of the community. The church board with which I was having a meeting in the fourth month of my pastorate consisted of an uneducated group of ladies. Only one of the members was employed, and she was the church treasurer (and the "church boss") who took great pride in her power. Something we were discussing that afternoon upset her to the point that she said, "I don't like what's going on here. I resign!"

Without thinking of what we would do without her leadership and her tithes, I spoke up and said to her, "I'm sorry you feel that way. I'll be by later this afternoon to pick up the books." With that, the power broker of Hohenwald got up and stalked out.

Silence filled the room as she left. Finally, someone spoke up and said, "She's been threatening to do that for years. It's time someone called her bluff."

I didn't mean to call her bluff. I just believed that the church belongs to God—not the dear departed sister. You have probably guessed the results. That little church went on a growing spree. Money came in to meet our needs. To this very day I'm not sure of its source. We experienced the best days in the history of the church.

Satan turned up the heat, but God cooled it down.

I have pastored for more than 40 years and have been in every size of community and church. Trust me—if you move into Satan's territory, he will fight back. Don't invade his neighborhood unless you are ready for battle. Remember: every pastorate has its own furnacelike experiences.

It is true that we pastors are not to "lord it over" our people. The person who would be a good pastor will have a servant's heart. Jesus said, "The greatest among you will be your servant. For whoever exalts himself will be humbled, and whoever humbles himself will be exalted" (Matt. 23:11-12).

There is to be a softness in us. However, it is not to be misconstrued as weakness. Quite the contrary. That softness, a servant's heart, brings us into closer identity with Him. And where He is, there is victory. Our strength is in His presence. Remember: "We are more than conquerors through him who loved us" (Rom. 8:37).

If you still have trouble believing in the conquering power of God, then reread the account of the Crucifixion. When Satan had done his worst (he had destroyed the Master, or so he thought), God the Father had a different idea—resurrection! I have often wondered if, following the wonderful victory of the Resurrection, Satan wished he had never done that. When we have His Spirit and His presence, we experience Resurrection-style victories.

Surely when Shadrach, Meshach, and Abednego came out of an overheated furnace without even the smell of smoke on their clothes, the devil realized his was not a good idea. And when King Nebuchadnezzar issued his new decree that anyone who spoke against the God of these three Hebrews would be cut to pieces, Satan knew he had committed a cardinal error.

Now how did this victory come to pass? The protective presence of the Son of God was in the furnace with those men. Our God can protect us from anything the devil throws at us. We can be triumphant regardless of how hostile the situation may be.

A number of years ago a member of my congregation made a sizable donation to get a building program going. The gift was just what we needed to get the congregation excited about the new project. Soon we were to the point of signing a contract for construction. The donor, who happened to be a member of the church board, wanted to name the contractor—or, perhaps I should say, "un-name" the contractor who had been selected by the board.

When he could not have his way, he tried to "pull the plug" on the building project. He underestimated the spirit of these people as they rallied and raised the funds to keep the project going. As the program progressed, he became increasingly furious. Someone had to be a sacrificial lamb. Guess who that would be? That's right—it was me!

A year later there was to be a pastoral vote by the congregation to determine if the relationship between the pastor and church should be continued.

This was the opportunity for him to get rid of me for not yielding to his wishes, even though I had not made the decision concerning the contractor—the board had.

On the week of the vote he kept the phone lines hot. On the Sunday of the election he and one of his cohorts were stopping people in the church parking lot to convince the people to vote against the pastor. (Carnality holds nothing sacred!) And they did succeed in convincing a large group of people to support their position. The balloting was completed, and the report came back with 382 yes and 78 no votes. Even though I could stay, for 78 people to say, "We really think you should leave," was very painful. At that time I was not aware of the "parking lot politics."

While the district superintendent preached, God and I had a serious conversation. He spoke first: "It hurts, doesn't it?"

"Lord, I've never had anything hurt like this," I responded. "I thought these people loved me."

"The Cross hurt too," He then said.

I had my answer. God had cooled the furnace for me. About that time a layman went to the ushers' phone and called the platform. "Pastor, I know how you feel," he said simply. "I just want you to know how much we love you."

All of a sudden the fire was nearly out. God was still in charge.

When the man who had stoked the furnace left town under a cloud, he called my wife and spent an hour and a half telling her what a sorry pastor I was. But he could not get the fire rekindled. There was no heat. It was he who was leaving—not I.

Remember: God is in charge of the heat in the furnaces of our lives.

Not all the heat we will experience comes from outside sources. I know of very few parsonage families who have not experienced some potentially destructive ordeals. Sickness, financial difficulty, or behavioral problems come to every one of us. And when they come, Satan will try to use these happenings to destroy us. You will hear these words: "If you were a good pastor . . ." or maybe even "If you were the Christian you profess to be . . ." He does everything possible to discourage us.

When walking through the valley of sorrows, we can expect to hear all kinds of noises. However, if we listen carefully, we will also hear the Prince of Peace say, "Let Me carry you for a while."

God has been unusually good in arranging my life. He knew just what I needed in order to make the most of what little talent I had. So when I was at the ripe age of 20, He brought Bettye Murray of Richmond, Kentucky, into my life. We were married for 39 years. During that period of time she got her Ph.T. (Putting Hubby Through) from Trevecca Nazarene College and Nazarene Theological Seminary. I acknowledged then, and I still do, that she was a wonderful pastor's wife.

I'll never forget when I was called to the Princeton, Florida, Church of the Nazarene. John L. Knight, the district superintendent, phoned me and said, "The Princeton Church has called Bettye to be the pastor's wife here."

I responded, "So what does that do with me?" He answered, "I guess you'll have to come with her." And for 10 years we worked side by side to build that great church.

Bettye continued to be a wonderful asset when we moved to Wichita, Kansas. For 19 years she worked among these parishioners, and they loved her.

It was no surprise, then, when following her untimely death in 1991, someone asked one of my children, "Will your father stay in the ministry?" They knew how vital she was to my pastoral role.

The furnace was hot. Now I had to decide if what I had shared with hundreds of families as I had stood on the other side of the casket was true. How is this going to work out? How can I minister to others with a wounded heart of my own?

After a year, I went away for a week to be totally alone with the Lord. He met me as I walked the beach of South Padre Island, Texas, and peace came. Before I could self-destruct, which some thought I would surely do, He came and cooled the furnace. He was still in charge.

In His kindness, God brought into my life another wonderful lady, Joyce McWhorter, who was on the staff of First Church of the Nazarene in Clearwater, Florida. How He brought us together is an incredible story in itself. We lived half a continent apart, but God arranged our meeting with each other through a wonderful young singer, Brian

Arner. God knew how to deliver me from the furnace. He wasn't through with me yet, so in His wisdom and kindness He brought Joyce and me together, and I was delivered from the furnace again. Now I'm playing second fiddle to another wonderful lady who is dearly loved and respected by the people of the same congregation.

There is one more family area where Satan really puts the heat on us, and that's with our children. When my youngest son, Pat, was a high school senior, Satan used him to turn up the heat in the furnace. Because of his desire now to give God the glory, Pat has encouraged me to share the story of how this furnace was brought under control.

Pat was a handsome, athletic, and very popular young man. He went to church every Sunday, but he struggled spiritually. And while we had what I considered to be a good camaraderie, at times our relationship was strained. I felt as though I had to lean hard on him to keep him in line. After all, I knew what was best for him (or so I thought), and I was only seeking his best interests. However, Pat didn't share my feelings.

At exactly midnight on the Saturday before Palm Sunday of 1987, he came into the bedroom, flipped on the light, and said, "Mom, Dad, I love you. Good-bye." I never saw the gun until after he fired it, shooting himself in the side with the full intention of taking his life.

Talk about fiery furnaces—this was the hottest it had ever become. It was 10 times hotter!

But God, as always, joined me in the furnace. I leaped out of bed and caught Pat before he fell. As

I was laying him down on the floor, God spoke very clearly to me: "He's not going to die." The voice was almost audible.

God did not speak to Bettye that night. Her experience came later. But I needed help right then, and God put the first layer of protection on me.

While we were awaiting the ambulance, God spoke to me again and said, "It's war! You are in a battle with Satan. While you are not vulnerable where money or moral temptations are concerned, you are very vulnerable where the kids are concerned. That's why Satan has struck here."

"Thank You, Lord," I whispered.

I had answers to two of the main questions that I would face. How was he?—He would not die. Why did this happen?—It was Satan's way of trying to defeat me.

The fire was under control. After Pat was stabilized at the hospital, I went home, rested awhile, went to church, and delivered the message God had given me. If God ever helped anyone, He helped me that day. This might be a good place to remember again the power, protection, and provision of a naive faith. I simply believed God.

Pat fully recovered, graduated from college, is serving the Lord with all his heart, and I am very, very proud of what he has accomplished. This may be a good place to remind parents who are struggling with their kids: hang on—keep praying—God is not through yet. Because, for me, the fire is out of that furnace!

In his beautiful book *Acts of Love,* pastor and author David Jeremiah has a chapter that should be read and reread by every pastor, titled "When All Else Fails." Jeremiah addresses the situation recorded in 1 Samuel 30 when David and his band of ragtag men were running from the army of King Saul.

David, his men, and their families had settled in Ziklag. The Amalekites came while David and his men were gone and burned the city, taking everyone captive. When David returned, he and his men wept until they had no more tears. It was such a devastating experience that the men wanted to stone David. But look at verse 6: "David strengthened himself in the LORD his God" (NASB).

The author writes, "There will be times when no one will be there for us but God."[1] Remember: God *is* there with you. He will encourage you, strengthen you, help you, and ultimately bring you out of your fiery furnace.

I remind you again that every life, especially that of a pastor, will have its seven-times-hotter-than-usual furnace experiences. But I also want to remind you not to be surprised when you sense a special Presence in the fire with you, absorbing the heat so that not even the smell of smoke will be on your clothes when you emerge.

And you will be delivered!

6
You're Not a Very Good Daddy!

I almost choked on the bite of food I had just eaten. My nine-year-old son, Steve, looked straight at me across the supper table and cut my heart out with six words. I had heard harsh criticism before, but those were the cruelest words that had ever been directed toward me.

"You're not a very good daddy," was the last thing I ever thought I would hear one of my kids say. But, the fact is—he was right.

I was head-over-heels in love with what I was doing—pastoring a very strong church in southern Florida. In addition to that, I was president of all youth ministries for the Florida District of our church, which at that time included the entire state, with the exception of the Panhandle. There was so much work to do with these 10,000 young people who were at a critical time in their lives, and I had a strong interest in helping them.

What I was doing was legitimate, but the price my family was paying was not.

Steve leveled those words at me while I was eating in a hurry so that I could go to West Palm Beach and minister to a group of those "needy" young people. However, I had not stopped to consider who was ministering to the "needy" children I had helped bring into the world. Shortly afterward, I left for my meeting.

On the way home that evening those words, "You're not a very good daddy," kept running through my mind. I honestly don't remember what I had preached or who or how many were there. My mind was in turmoil.

As He has done so often, God in His kindness came to my rescue. He began to explain what was going on and why these words of challenge had come from the mouth of my child. Our conversation was clear and simple. He spoke first, asking, "What day are you taking off from work to give your body a break?"

I answered, "Monday, Lord. You know I meet the fellows and play golf, relax, and recover from the exhaustion of Sunday. By Tuesday I'm renewed and can drive on through the week."

He then asked, "What day are the children out of school?"

I responded, "Saturday, Lord. But that's such a

great day for calling. I round up a lot of people on Saturday."

Then He replied, "I know you do. But where is your primary mission field?"

I got the message very quickly. If I reached a multitude of others at the expense of my own children, I had made a poor bargain.

God wasn't through with me yet. For He asked, "What day do you need to be at your best?"

"Sunday, Lord," I replied.

"So why don't you take Saturdays off, rest your body, spend time with your children?" He said. "Then you can be at your best on Sunday."

I had never won an argument with God, so why should I expect that I could do so now?

I listened, got the message, and changed my schedule. Since that Friday night in 1964 I have tried to make Saturday a time to rest physically and mentally as well as have fun with my family. This may not work for everyone, but it has been wonderful for me.

In my situation it was a matter of priorities, and I'm glad I made that decision. We have had some wonderful times. In fact, our home has been a very active part of "the zoo." Some people thought it was an integral part. Not far from our south Florida parsonage was a tourist attraction called

"Monkey Jungle." I can't tell you how many of my friends who knew our family asked if that was the parsonage!

I think I became a "good daddy" whose kids enjoyed growing up. That Friday night, driving home and listening to God, I determined to make whatever adjustments needed to be made. There are some priceless priorities that need to be protected and preserved. Believe me—the results have been more than worth the adjustments I made in my schedule. All our kids are now deeply involved in the work of the Kingdom.

One of the most pleasant and exciting areas of this zoo that we call ministry is the place where our families live. Every zoo I have ever visited has a serpentarium. Ours was no different. Yes, we had snakes in the house, and after one near-tragic experience, Bettye adjusted by learning how to handle them.

I have to explain that our sons Rick and Steve had a fascination for these curious creatures of God. They were all around our house, which was located in a semirural area in south Florida. The abundance of lush undergrowth was inhabited by many snakes of varied species.

The second week we lived there, a pygmy rattlesnake crawled across the kitchen floor. Then there was the garter snake that lived in the planter in our living room. That's the one that called for a reorganizing of Bettye's priorities.

When our district superintendent, John L. Knight, came for a visit, I gathered the kids in the living room to visit with our distinguished guest. I wanted them to get to know him and think of him as a friend. Dr. Knight was sitting in front of the planter telling stories and regaling the kids with his unique personality. I didn't see it, but Bettye did. Rick's pet snake that had escaped earlier climbed up one of the plants that was right behind the dear doctor's head. He was not aware of the drama taking place. Bettye looked fiery daggers at Rick. She had told him earlier to find the snake and put it away. She mouthed to him, "You're dead!"

Rick immediately got the message and excused himself ostensibly to go to the bathroom. As he passed the planter, he surreptitiously grabbed the snake and took it out. Our honored guest never knew what had happened.

Wanting to be a good mother, Bettye said to Rick, "If you're going to have those things in the house, you have to teach me how to handle them." Remember, good parents do everything they can to help their children feel loved. I truly believe that parents of P.K.s (preacher's kids) especially need to practice this—although you may not need to go as far as Bettye did!

Soon after Bettye became a "snake handler," there was a bridal shower at the parsonage. One of the games they played required a blindfolded person to identify certain objects with her bare feet. After the usual assortment of peeled grapes, spaghetti, and so on, Bettye decided to show off her new talent. The ladies in attendance could not believe their eyes when their dignified pastor's wife went to the planter and brought out the snake. When the victim could not guess what this item was and removed her blindfold, she almost went into cardiac arrest.

To this day, the ladies who were there point to that shower as one of the most entertaining ones ever. And, yes, we were able to continue pastoring there!

Speaking of becoming a "good daddy," I had some more adjusting to do with my only daughter, Laurel. One day I walked into her tiny bedroom (and I do mean *tiny*), and Laurel was lying on her bunk looking at the walls and the ceiling, counting something. I asked curiously, "What are you doing?"

"I'm counting my horses," she replied. I knew then that we had a serious problem. Here was my lovely 12-year-old daughter hallucinating over nonexistent horses.

I had never had anything to do with horses. So why did Laurel have this fascination with those big creatures that cost a lot, eat a lot, and need a lot of room? Why couldn't she just love dogs or even cats? Why horses?

I never learned the answer to that question, but I did learn to have some feelings for her first love. The following Christmas a member of our congregation who was a horse lover helped me bring "Cocoa" into our family. A neighbor provided a pasture for this young mare, and Laurel could now actually count one horse.

They became inseparable. When my "horse lady" got home from school, the first thing she did was to go to her "first love." She bathed that horse with our garden hose and rode her every day. I thought I had solved a major problem by giving my daughter this meaningful creature to share her life.

Then the whole idea became extremely complicated. I was called to pastor First Church of the Nazarene in Wichita, Kansas. That was halfway across the continent. When I told the kids we were moving, Laurel's first question was, "What about Cocoa?"

I responded, "We'll get her out there." Frankly, I really thought we should sell her and get another horse in Kansas.

We had been in Wichita a couple of months when Laurel asked, "When is Cocoa coming?" I then tried to convince her to sell Cocoa and buy a new horse. She wasn't buying *that!* She responded, "But, Dad, you promised!" And she was right. I *had* promised. So is my word any good? I wanted her to believe what I preached, and if I didn't deliver, my credibility would be destroyed. I was not about to run that risk. So I found a friend who was going to Florida to pick up some horses. He did indeed have room for one more.

While it cost more to move that horse than I had paid for her, I wanted to be a "good daddy" in whom Laurel could believe. I was willing to do anything to keep my word. So on a bitter-cold January day, this four-legged animal that had been basking in the balmy breezes of southern Florida arrived in Wichita—enabling me to continue making my special corner of the zoo happy.

I don't mean to imply that we always succeeded in delighting our kids. There were times when being good parents required making one or the other of the children unhappy.

Bettye was the organist for the Princeton Church. She and Brent, our three-year-old, sat on the front pew close to the instrument. One Sunday evening when God had moved on the hearts of the people, many in the congregation came forward to pray and do serious business with the Lord. Bettye went to the altar to counsel with one of the ladies after giving Brent strict orders to not leave the pew. He didn't—he didn't have to.

After a few minutes of prayer and serious soul-searching, a ghastly "bla-a-ah!" came from the organ. It startled everyone. Brent had discovered that he could reach the bass notes of the organ without leaving his pew and decided to amuse himself in that manner.

After she got over her start, his mother looked at him, shook her finger, and mouthed, "Don't do that again!"

She went back to her altar work.

You're getting ahead of me, but you're right. He did it again! "Bla-a-ah!" Some of the people snickered; Bettye fumed. She caught his eye again and said those words that should strike fear to any child's heart: "Don't you dare do that again, or you've had it!"

She again returned to her counseling and had no more than recovered from the interruption when it was charm time—that is, if you believe the third time is a charm. "Bla-a-ah!" For all practical purposes, that altar service was over. This cat-and-mouse game had some laughing and others wondering why we couldn't control our kids. Well, the cat got the mouse this time. Bettye left the altar, swept Brent onto her shoulder, and headed for the back door.

Jesse Underwood was sitting three pews behind the site of the drama and later gave me this account. He could hardly talk for laughing as he quoted the words Brent prayed as Bettye hurriedly carried him up the aisle: "O Lord! O Lord! Please help me—she whips *so* hard!"

Apparently the discipline took. Brent is now a career police officer in Overland Park, Kansas. Recently he and his family were founding members of a new church in that area.

Sometimes you have to laugh to keep from crying. When our youngest son, Pat, was in the fourth grade, he came home from school early one day. Upon entering the house, he found his mother running the vacuum in a small, narrow hallway. Realizing that she did not know he was there, Pat slipped up behind her and grabbed her around the waist. He decided to test his manly strength by lifting his mother off the floor. He found out he wasn't yet a man as they both toppled over backward onto the floor, with Bettye on top of this would-be weight lifter. The fall hurt her back so badly that she couldn't get up, and Pat thought he was going to die. They almost did—they practically laughed themselves to death as they struggled to get up and couldn't.

I know it may sound weird, but that experience of laughing themselves silly is one of Pat's most memorable moments. And why not? Zoos are fun for laypersons and clergy, and our kids need to know that.

Good parents teach their children to take responsibility and to make serious decisions.

In attempts to be a "good daddy," I have endeavored to instruct this also.

We had a female mutt that had brought great pleasure to our family. In fact, Cookie, as we affectionately called her, brought more than pleasure to us—she delivered 93 puppies over those years to our parsonage. (No lectures, please!) It's too bad we couldn't count them for Sunday School, but that's not relevant to this story and its lesson.

On Christmas Eve during Cookie's 10th year as a part of our zoo, she was obviously quite ill. Rick and I tenderly loaded her into the car for a visit to the veterinarian. The doctor checked her over carefully, then looked at us and said, "She's in bad shape. You really should put her to sleep." He went on to explain that she had cancer and some other problems that were typical of old dogs that lived outdoors in south Florida.

Rick's face fell to the floor. Here it was Christmas Eve, and the doctor was telling us to put this beloved dog to sleep. How can you think of Christmas and losing something you love dearly at the same time?

I told Rick that the decision was his. I would do whatever he wanted to do. He asked the vet if there wasn't something that could be done. The vet said, "No. The best thing I know to do is to put her out of her misery."

Tears welled up in my young son's eyes as he pondered his decision. Then he asked, "Can we take her home and think about it?"

I told him again. "It's your decision."

We thanked the vet, took our beloved Cookie, and returned home. That afternoon Rick talked to a neighbor lady and shared the family's immediate crisis. This wise neighbor told him to give the dog some aspirin to keep her comfortable. He did. And Cookie became so comfortable that she lived another year and had one more litter of pups!

I would never have made the decision Rick made. I did, however, make a better one. I trusted him to do the right thing, which he did, and then I supported him with love. That is being a good daddy.

Our kids are not perfect. As I have recalled in other places, some of their decisions all but broke our hearts. Still, with love, kindness, patience, and some willingness to adjust the priorities of our lives, we can all become "good daddies."

7
FRIENDLY KEEPERS

"Pastor, I've been wanting to do this for a long time. I want you to know how much my family and I love and appreciate you." And with that, my "keeper" slid across the table a box containing a beautiful watch.

I was overwhelmed by this expression of love and caring. It was one of those very special moments that occasionally come my way. It also brought to mind occasions in the past when I sat at some not-so-friendly tables. In fact, there were times when I was unable to share a meal because I felt as though *I* was the meal! That explains why this moment was so special to me. It was at the other end of the spectrum. God has a wonderful way of balancing out all our experiences.

Of course, I am fully aware that many pastors

are never treated to major expressions of love and appreciation. A great number of churches do not have laypersons who possess resources to do these things. But if we look carefully, almost any pastor who has stayed at his or her assignment for a reasonable period of time has had some "keepers" who made the stay in the "zoo" pleasant.

While pastoring the little community church in Mirabile, Missouri, during my years in seminary, I learned how "pastor conscious" some laypersons are. Early one Friday morning I received a call informing me that an elderly gentleman in the congregation had died and that the funeral was to be held Sunday at 11 A.M. I could hardly believe my ears—that was the scheduled time for our morning worship service. Why would they plan a funeral at the church for this time on Sunday morning? Then I was informed that these plans had been made because of the heat and the expected response of elderly people. The funeral service needed to be held in the coolest part of the day. Their reasoning became clear. It was July, and our little unair-conditioned church was in the middle of a Missouri wheat field, a formula for unbearable afternoon heat. Still, the arrangements created some problems for me.

In the first place, this would be my premier funeral sermon, and my seminary studies had not yet covered that assignment. In the second place, my remuneration for driving 130 miles round-trip and spending the entire day in the country was whatever came in for the offering. I had no guaranteed salary. Sometimes the response was good; sometimes it was not so good—but at least there was always something. And we needed all the help we could get. With two small children, it seemed unwise for Bettye to work outside the home. I was in quite a quandary. How do you take an offering at a funeral? But then, if we *didn't* take an offering, how could we make ends meet?

With the special grace of God, I was able to get through the funeral. As a matter of fact, I still have that outline. I well remember the ladies' duet and the graveside service, where we stayed until the body was lowered and the grave filled with dirt. That is an experience in itself, and I shall never forget it.

Concerning the other problem, I had decided to let this be a day of helping others. Never mind our financial needs. Sure, attending seminary and parenting two small children certainly stretched our budget. But I knew we would be all right. Somehow things would work out.

While musing this over in my mind, a layman slipped up to me, handed me an envelope, and said, "Pastor, we didn't get to take the offering this morning. Here's my tithe."

One after another they came to me until, by the end of the day, the offering was one of our best. God had indeed more than met our needs. These laypersons were "pastor conscious," and they took care of us. Frankly, I was glad for the situation the funeral created. It was a very special thing to feel the love and concern of our people. That just may have been one of the best lessons I learned at seminary.

I have an idea that there are very few pastors who have stayed in an assignment long enough to become the "shepherd of the flock" who cannot look back at that pastorate and point to a similar instance when the people did something very special. It may have been money, clothing, a meal, or just a nice card expressing appreciation. But the gift had love written all over it.

Many of these warm fuzzy experiences for me have come when Satan was trying to cause despair. You can be sure that when you move into the enemy's territory he will try to find some way to defeat you. If nothing else, he wants to break your concentration on the work of the Kingdom.

If we stay focused, God will provide whatever we need, whether it be money or a fresh awareness that our people love us.

While working on this book, I received a phone call from a former member who had moved to another state.

"Pastor," he said, "God has been waking me up in the middle of the night to pray for you. How are things going?"

I admitted to being very weary and wrestling with some heavy decisions. He replied, "I just wanted you to know that I love you. I'll keep praying for you." Once again, God had given me some needed strokes from a friendly keeper.

I wonder why it still amazes and surprises me to see how God takes care of His people. Those of us who are pastors have a habit of forgetting that what we preach to those wonderful people who sit on the other side of the pulpit also applies to those who stand behind it. It helps to remember that there is only one standard for all of God's people.

That means that God not only knows and cares about what is going on in their lives but also knows and cares about what is happening in ours. We can be sure that God weighs every experience we face in the scales of His divine love. When needed, He steps in to make a difference. In my life, He has used the wonderful people I have pastored to counter the enemy's attacks on many occasions.

During the early years of my pastoral ministry, when we lived from payday to payday, there was never any surplus. Many times there were not sufficient funds to pay all our bills on time. I learned to call our creditors and get extensions on loans. With no savings account and, for many of those years, no credit cards, you will understand when I tell you that Christmas for five children was a problem. I'm not talking about getting them extravagant gifts. I'm talking about getting them *any* gifts at all. There were times when I took a cheap, shaggy Christmas tree and wired extra branches into it to make it look better. We made many of our own decorations, and I once made the string of lights for our tree.

The only good thing about our situation was that we have always pastored churches in which there were some loving, caring laypersons. I remind you that not all of them loved us, but most of them did.

For most of those early years we pastored in churches where the people practiced the beautiful habit of taking a Christmas love offering for the pastoral family. In churches with multiple staff members, this would be very difficult. But I never had staff until I became the pastor of Wichita First Church. So we were the recipients of Christmas love offerings for many years.

Bettye and I came to count on this wonderful expression of love to provide the means for our Christmas shopping for the family. That made the Sunday before Christmas very special to us. These offerings have ranged from a few dollars in small churches (where a money tree had 32 one-dollar bills attached) to some very generous gifts in recent years.

Fortunately for us, in one of our churches there were some people in leadership who didn't like me. Now don't faint—get the whole story!

In this church the privilege of taking the love offering belonged to an "unfriendly" keeper, who happened to be the same person who had strongly encouraged me to leave. So when Christmastime came, he decided to get at me by "protecting my dignity." He determined that it was degrading for the pastor to sit there while the offering plates were being passed. So he arranged for a more dignified gift—a briefcase—along with appropriate "nice" words.

The problem was that the briefcase was empty, and we had absolutely nothing with which to purchase gifts for the children. As we left church that day, I was "dignified" but concerned about our financial needs. I should have remembered that there was no need to be concerned—God was still in charge.

That afternoon, one after another the kind, loving people of that church came by the parsonage. One was an older farmer who said, "Pastor, I don't know why the love offering wasn't taken this morning. We've always done something special for our pastor and family." Then he generously placed a folded green bill in my hand.

I learned later that there was no organized effort. They just wanted to say, "We love you and your family." When it was all over, that was one of our best Christmas experiences ever. There were some very friendly keepers at that zoo.

It is important to realize that kindness and love do not always involve money or gifts of some kind.

Sometimes a phone call or a note of appreciation and support is just as important (or even more so) than a monetary expression. Or perhaps it may be a special privilege that is given.

Dr. Louis Morgan, a member of our church, has a large farm with several peaceful fishing ponds. He has very kindly extended to us "fishing rights." On many days when the pressure has been intense, Joyce and I go to a pond in the evening and find a tranquil oasis.

On such an evening, we had just rowed out onto the lake when I caught my first fish. Scarcely had I reeled it in before Joyce also caught one. Now she can catch them, but she won't take them off the hook! So I was wrestling with two live fish in the bottom of that boat. Before I knew it, the hook on one of the lures had wedged itself deeply in my finger. There was a fish on one end of the lure wriggling to get loose and I was on the other end wishing *I* could get loose. Slowly we rowed back to shore and drove to Dr. Morgan's house.

The good doctor carefully tried to extract the hook in his kitchen. But it was too firmly embedded. So we had to go to his office. This very friendly keeper extended more than his hospitality—he also took care of me in his off-duty time. And his wife rode with us, praying all the way. We were all amazed at how quickly that wound healed. Even though we had interrupted their quiet evening, they still encouraged us to come back again to enjoy the fun of fishing.

We have friends in Joyce's hometown, Roanoke, Virginia, who built a lovely home in a picturesque hilltop setting that is specifically designed for entertaining. They purposefully planned a suite and other guest rooms as a retreat for weary pastors, missionaries, evangelists, and others who need a respite from life's storms. What a delight it has been to enjoy their extraordinary hospitality!

A lot of encouragement comes in simpler ways. I have kept a "warm fuzzy" file of cards and letters that I go to for a lift on those occasions when I get to feeling a little low. In fact, as I write these lines I lift my eyes to see a card I received several years ago when Bettye died. It came months after the deluge of sympathy cards had ended and the reality of living alone had settled in. Let me share with you this beautiful card, complete with the note. God was again providing just the encouragement I needed to give me a few "strokes."

Card message:

I wonder if you realize what a good example you are for others. The wonderful way you live your life, the unconditional kindness you show to others, all the things that you do and that you are, touch the lives of the people around you. You are so sincere in your beliefs, so determined to be the sort of person God wants us to be, that people are inspired by you. They see the satisfaction you get from your faith, from having the courage of your convictions, and it helps them to try and live the same way. It's all such a wonderful tribute to you and your way of life that I just had to tell you so. God must be very proud of you.

—Dale Wildman*

Personal note:

Read it again! It's everything you are. We love you and continue to hold you up in prayer.

Paul and Kathy

Again, I thank God for friendly keepers. And there are many of them in every zoo.

Fellow pastors, open your ears and listen—open your eyes to see what is really happening.

Laymen—you can be a real encouragement to your pastor as he wages war against Satan. Friendly keepers enable weary pastors to stay in the battle and in the zoo!

---

*© 1988 Hallmark, Inc. Reprinted by permission.

8
NOBODY'S PERFECT

"Gene. This is Pastor Lyle. Where are you?"

The sound of my friend's voice coming from my answering machine quickened my pulse. Only then did I remember that I was scheduled to speak for a special citywide crusade in Udall, Kansas. That commitment had not crossed my mind for a number of days. What had been intended to be a fun-filled evening with a group of believers from every church in this little town located about 20 miles southeast of Wichita had suddenly become an embarrassing nightmare for me, as well as for my friend, Lyle.

I had just stood up an entire town! They had erected a tent and spent the night roasting a pig. Their plans had been made for a full day of "old-fashioned fun" to be climaxed under the tent with a service of praise and preaching. I was the preacher, and I had just plain forgotten the assignment. That is, without a doubt, one of the most embarrassing moments of my entire life.

So what do you do when you blow it?

When you are involved in ministry you *will*, sometime when you least need to, make an embarrassing mistake.

Unfortunately, there are some ministers who have the crazy idea that they have to be letter perfect. You know what I mean. We have all met them —these prodigies of perfection. They believe every hair must be in place, their appearance must always be color-coordinated, every "t" must be crossed, and every "i" must be dotted. They put themselves under pressure not only to look right but also to say everything just right. They have no margin of error, and they pay dearly for this fetish that possesses them.

Such people play right into the devil's hands. You can be sure that he will see to it that something goes wrong. And he will make them think that the mistake is so critical that there is no credibility with the parishioners. Satan makes them want to crawl into a hole and hide. I know. I have dug some holes. Thank goodness, I never stayed in them very long.

I believe that there is no place in the ministry for sloppy carelessness either in appearance or in performance of duty. It is essential that pastors look and act the very best that is possible. For those of us in the ministry, our assignment calls us to be at our very best. However, to put such a premium on perfection that our humanity is stifled is a drastic mistake. Ministers are human, and human beings make mistakes. So maybe some pastors need to "lighten up."

God in His kindness has helped me face my very imperfect humanity. I can honestly say that I try to do the best job possible.

I want the Master and my people to be proud to be associated with me.

However, I have a clear realization that none of us is faultless, and I will not be in bondage to a lifestyle that demands perfection.

I relate well to an ad that is directed to those who wear dentures. The punchline says, "Fixodent —and forget it."

So when I make a blunder, I fix it, forget it, and through God's grace, move on. Some of my people would add ". . . to the next blooper!"

When I realized that I had stood up the city of Udall, I was embarrassed to the core. How could I adequately apologize to my friend Lyle, who had lovingly invited me? What would those people think? Our morning worship service is broadcast on the radio in that area, and many of them were listeners. Would they ever again listen with confidence?

I told my wife, Joyce: "We're going to Udall. I can't just call and say I forgot. I have to look those people in the eyes and apologize."

On our way, Joyce asked, "How many people will be there? How large is Udall?"

I responded, "It was for the entire town, and there are 2,500 people who live there."

She really got nervous then, for she assumed along with me that most of the 2,500 would be there. Fortunately for me, *not* the entire town showed up.

Just as we pulled up to the city park where the meeting was to have been held, we saw the tent coming down. My stomach was churning. I had to find Lyle and let him "tell me off."

I found my friend. He didn't cut me to pieces. Rather, he loved me even when I told him I had just plain forgotten the assignment. He smiled and said, "We were afraid you'd been involved in an accident. We're relieved that you're all right. Come on—have some of the hog we smoked."

Incredibly, I was forgiven. God had helped them to have a good time without a preacher. They had enjoyed good music, and God had honored them with His presence—a more-than-adequate replacement for mine!

Now I can forget it—except to learn from the experience. Now both my secretary and my wife have my schedule so that I am reminded twice every day of each appointment.

I wish I could say that was the only mistake I have made in these 40-plus years. However, you and I both know better. Anyone who lives in the public eye is—I repeat—*is* going to make some mistakes. We just have to hope and pray that they are not too embarrassing and that the people who observe those "goofs" accept us as human beings.

That's the key point.

Since we are human, we should not present ourselves to those to whom we minister as anything more.

If we attempt to elevate ourselves above the human level, then we will be expected to perform above that level—and that's a scary thought.

Can we be God's person and still be a very human human being? Elijah was. Yet we find this man of God in a less-than-perfect condition. Notice how he is described in 1 Kings 19:3-4: "Elijah was afraid and ran for his life. When he came to Beersheba in Judah, he left his servant there, while he himself went a day's journey into the desert. He came to a broom tree, sat down under it and prayed that he might die. 'I have had enough, LORD,' he said. 'Take my life; I am no better than my ancestors.'"

Elijah, God's man, was afraid. He was so discouraged that he wanted to die. That's not the attitude of a perfect person. But who of us would not be pleased to be considered the man of God Elijah was?

Again, I want to emphasize that there is no room for lazy, sloppy carelessness. God wants and deserves our very best in every area of living. But

don't give Satan the club of "perfection" with
which to beat you. He has enough weapons to use.

One of the easiest places to make mistakes is in
the pulpit. That is especially true for those of us
who do not read our sermons from manuscripts.
On occasion, my congregation will break out in
laughter at something I have said. Most of the time
I never even realize what has happened. It works
better that way, for when I'm caught in a "blooper,"
my face turns as red as a fire truck. I can't help
blushing, and my people love it when they get a
chance to laugh at their pastor.

Thankfully, God has given me the disposition
to laugh at myself. Why not? What else can one do
when he has used the word that is the exact opposite of what was intended? My people have very
vivid imaginations. On at least two occasions I have
innocently used phrases that conjure some very embarrassing mental pictures. While they choke back
the laughter, I have continued preaching, totally
oblivious to the mistake until presented a tape of
the message. I can hardly believe I said those
things. Even more amazing, they allow me to stay
and continue preaching!

I grew up under the ministry of H. H. Wise,
who pastored First Church of the Nazarene in
Nashville for 26 years. After he had made one of
those infamous errors, I can remember Pastor Wise
saying he wished he had a trap door behind the
pulpit so he could push a button and disappear. I
can certainly relate to that.

I believe one of the reasons Pastor Wise was
able to stay at that assignment for so long was his

humanity. He was a scholar, teacher, and great preacher. But he was far from perfect. Consequently, the people could relate to him. They loved him for his humanity.

It has been said, "Honest confession is good for the soul." One of my most recent "foot-in-the-mouth" incidents occurred after a Sunday morning worship service. A new couple to our church paused to shake hands with me. After greeting the wife, I turned to the young-looking man behind her and said, "This must be your son."

Very coldly, she replied, "I don't know what you mean." It finally dawned on me that this was her husband. "I believe I just said the wrong thing," I then told her.

"You certainly did," she promptly replied. In a huff (and I don't blame her), they marched off. I feel quite confident that I will never see them again. It certainly was not my best day for "winning friends and influencing people."

I have come to a realization, however, that really helps me with my bumbling blunders. It's hard for people to relate to perfection. We can respect and even admire it, but since most of us are quite imperfect, we relate best to those who are honest enough to allow their humanity to show.

Another one of the kinks in my armor is tunnel vision. (You may recall the young nursing mother at the Hohenwald church I mentioned earlier.) This is the tendency to see neither what is left or right but to focus on what is straight ahead. Add to this the fact that I do not hear well, and you will understand why sometimes this places me in potentially embarrassing situations. Occasionally, I give the wrong answer when I guess at the question someone has asked. Other times I walk right by people who have spoken to me. This happens most often when I am making my way to the pulpit. The corridor is crowded, the people are talking, and I simply did not hear—or hear correctly. So I blunder on toward the platform, and someone is left with a very puzzled look.

On occasion I have made public apologies. For, you see, I really understand that I am a long way from being perfect. I am working to broaden my vision—but the hearing aid is something my pride is going to have to deal with.

There is wisdom in letting people know that we are aware of our imperfection. When we accept and acknowledge this, I believe it enables the people to love their human pastor.

While working on this book, I had one of those experiences that could easily ruin a Sunday morning. Joyce was out of town. As I made my way to church, I decided to get a large cup of coffee to go. I placed it in the cup holder in my Jeep and began the process of slowly waking up as I made my way to church.

Just as I turned the corner one block from the church, I was quickly awakened—the cup turned over in my lap. There I sat in a leather seat with a lap full of hot coffee. Worse yet, my suit was a mess, and I wondered what everyone would speculate about the stains.

Fortunately, I have a habit of getting to the church at least an hour before the service. So if I decided to, I could rush home, change, and rush back feeling frustrated that my routine was messed up. Or I could hope that the coffee would dry up and my dark suit would not show the stains.

I opted for the latter, feeling that my mental frame of mind was more important than my physical appearance. A proper attitude was more critical than a crease in my pants. Since God in His kindness has released me from the bondage of perfectionism, I was able to make the right decision.

Somehow, my early morning coffee encounter slipped into the message, and my people enjoyed a good laugh with their very human pastor. Furthermore, I am now the proud owner of two spill-proof coffee cups—courtesy of some sympathetic members.

No one in my congregation ridiculed or criticized me. No one left the church because their pastor is less than perfect. Rather, they related to my sleepiness in that early hour. In fact, it was easy for them to understand fully that I am very human. And they certainly appreciate that I recognized I am not perfect and do not pretend to be.

The army has an ad that challenges us, "Be all that you can be—in the army." I echo the challenge to be all that you can be. But remember: nobody's perfect. Do not let anyone or anything put you under that kind of pressure.

I could regale you with story after story—blooper after blooper. Suffice it to say that when I make the statement "Nobody's perfect," I am speaking to myself first.

The road to a happy ministry is paved
with the realization that after I have done
my best, by God's grace and through the
kindness of my people,
I can live with the mistakes that
are made along the way.

9
KEEPING FRESH IN DRY TIMES

He was six feet, five inches tall, weighed 325 pounds, and had arms as big as my thighs. Still, I felt a strong sense of empathy with John. As he sat resting on a chair after pouring himself into a service, he looked me straight in the eyes and asked, "Pastor, you've been at this for over 40 years. How  do you stay fresh? You seem to have found a way to keep going."

God was using this gentle giant to win souls for the Kingdom as he fulfilled the role of an evangelist. Even though he was incredibly big, he was physically and emotionally drained after the activities of that evening. He used tremendous feats of strength to get the attention of the people. Then, clearly and concisely, he presented the message of God's Word. Now he was exhausted. "I don't want to burn out like so many evangelists have done," he went on to say.

At least this big hunk of human flesh recognized such a danger. In spite of the great physical strength he possessed, he was a candidate for self-destruction.

The truth is—*most* ministers are. Unfortunately, many pastors are not aware of this insidious danger. Because of the divine hand that rests upon us, many of us get the crazy idea that we are indestructible. This creates a drain on our energy that will result in major problems unless it is acknowledged and faced honestly. Often it's too late by the time we recognize our mistaken judgment.

Look around you at this journey of faith. Sadly, you will find it littered with spiritual, emotional, and even physical casualties.

Something is wrong. Why are there so many wasted messengers of God's Word? Why have so many of the 900 sincere students with whom I rubbed shoulders during three years of seminary dried up and been blown away? There must be a reason why so many of them "dehydrated" spiritually.

I have some very dear friends who were brilliant students and who grew wonderfully in their early "plantings" as pastors. Unfortunately, they have become spiritual wrecks. This happened because they did not acknowledge their own limitations and the dangers that await all of God's people.

In their book *Pastors at Risk,* H. B. London Jr. and Neil Wiseman write:

> Even emotionally robust pastors find it takes lots of energy and large doses of patience to simultaneously cope with whining traditionalists, demanding baby boomers, and lethargic church members. And in times of tight budgets and declining volunteerism, some congregations increase the pastor's burden by expecting him to deal with trivia, like folding bulletins or cutting the grass.
>
> As a result, a perpetual pastoral juggling act is required to deal with the mushrooming expectations that originate from spouse, children, congregation, denomination, community, or even self. To jumble the issues even more, these expectations often conflict with each other.
>
> As a result, a dehumanizing fatigue of faithfulness becomes a way of life for too many pastors. Unfinished tasks dog them, so they are never free from omnipresent demands—at dinner, on the basketball court, on days off, or in tender moments with spouse or children. Even the strong feel their stamina wearing thin.[1]

On the farm of one of our members, I had a two-acre garden plot for a number of years. It provided fresh vegetables at a time when we were feeding three children. And that was nice. But more important, it provided a place for me to get alone with God and away from everything else. To get to my garden I had to drive through the woods and ford the creek. It was wonderful. I spent many late afternoons and Saturdays listening to the chirping of the birds, the babbling of the creek, and the wind blowing through the trees. As I pulled weeds, picked veggies, and toiled in the hot sun, sometimes the sweat dripped from my body. It was a wonderfully peaceful practice for me.

It can get very hot in July in Kansas. Even though my garden sanctuary was close to a creek and shade, working there could take its toll on my body's moisture. And that's what happened to me late one July afternoon.

In my haste to get to my garden, I had neglected to take any drinking water with me. After working hard, I began to sweat freely. (Yes, I don't perspire—I *sweat!* And, yes, it's OK for preachers to sweat.) I began to feel dizzy.

Fortunately for me, my farmer friend came by and recognized what was happening. He recognized that I was flirting with a heatstroke. He made me move into the shade, drink some water, and rest awhile. In a few minutes I regained my strength and went back to work. You can be sure that from then on I was careful to bring a jug of water along.

We recognize the need to take care of our physical bodies. In fact, sports drinks that replenish and refresh athletes have become a major business. So why don't we understand the need to have our spiritual lives replenished? Why do so many go into spiritual dehydration?

Maybe such pastors are like a football coach I had in high school. He was from the old school, and I do mean *old*. There was no water on our practice field. We had to get into shape and become real men. "Get tough!" he said.

Looking back, I'm not sure if the reason we never had a winning season was because of our lack of ability or his lack of common sense. There is nothing manly about being thirsty to the bone!

I have an idea that there are ministers who are drying up unnecessarily. They have heard someone (probably Satan) ridicule any program of recreation and restoration. They may, as one young minister I knew, believe that they must always be in prayer or some other heavy activity. It's no surprise that this minister is no longer in the pastorate. Am I saying there is something wrong with prayer? You know better. It wasn't his activities—it was his attitude that drove him out.

It is no fun ministering from a dry heart, a dehydrated mind, and an exhausted body. Satan knows that, and if he can steer a man or woman of God into that condition, you had better believe he will.

My friend, John the gentle giant, seemed to think I had found a way to keep from growing spiritually and mentally stale. And I believe he's right.

> ## I am convinced that one of the best things God did for me is give me the ability to know and acknowledge my limitations.

The Father has endowed me with the common sense to admit when I become aware that I'm being stretched thin physically, emotionally, or spiritually—and then to do something about it. I understand that there are no superhuman preachers. Common sense tells us to acknowledge our humanity. And I believe I do that.

I have several places to retreat when I need to be alone. On numerous occasions I have spent time alone in some quiet places. While I'm there, my time is occupied with reading and listening to Him. Many times when the work and pressures begin to close in on me, I head for my garden spot simply to unclutter my mind. There is something therapeutic for me about pulling weeds and picking fruit.

Perhaps God has been exceptionally kind to me, but I have no illusions about being superhuman. I understand and acknowledge my weakness and have the wisdom to seek help.

A year after Bettye died, some very kind friends made an apartment at the beach available to me. I spent a week reading, sleeping, praying, sleeping, walking the beach, sleeping. I think you get the picture. I went there emotionally and physically drained. I came back renewed and restored to life again.

There have been other times when I simply get into the car and ride into the country. The static in my mind clears so that I'm able to hear the Master's voice. Sometimes I listen to music as I ride the back roads. But most of the time I just listen to God.

Certainly, every minister needs some physical exercise routine. Years ago, as a young minister, l heard that Billy Graham jogged to rid himself of some of his tension. So I began to jog and work out. It didn't make me into a Billy Graham, but I did run off a lot of stress.

I understand that no two of us are alike. Therefore, our interests and abilities will vary. My good friend Edmund Nash relaxes by listening to classical music. It soothes and restores him. For me, an ol' Nashville boy, I relax best with southern gospel. The point is—everyone must have some way to get away from things for a while. Jesus said to His followers in Mark 6:31: "Come ye yourselves apart . . . and rest a while" (KJV). We are His followers today. Shouldn't we do likewise?

Another way to stay fresh is to keep our minds renewed. Each pastor must always remember that each week has a Sunday and Wednesday. For me that has meant over 1,500 speaking assignments. Frankly, I long ago ran out of the vast store of knowledge I had when leaving the seminary. Still, those Sundays and Wednesdays keep rolling around. So, how do you keep the well from running dry? You keep putting something into it.

I shamefully confess a period when I was not reading much. As a consequence, I grabbed my share of Saturday night specials. Sometimes they worked out, but more often they did not. All I did was fill the preaching time in that service. I gave the people a sermon—not a message from God. Truthfully, the fact that I knew I was not ready was frightening and energy-draining. I had the whole responsibility for the service, and that is an awesome load. Maturity, more reading, and better preparation habits not only have provided better messages for my people but also have made the ministry of preaching more enjoyable for me. And the more pleasure there is in any activity, the less stressful and exhausting it becomes.

Being at my present assignment for over 24 years has really caused me to keep digging for sermon material. I make it a habit to read a minimum of two books a month. The more I put into my mind and heart, the more I have to share.

Remember: you cannot give out in the presentation of God's message what you have not taken in from other sources.

I fully recognize the need to be anointed of God in the pulpit. But the idea of "Lord, fill my mouth with worthwhile stuff, and nudge me when I've said enough" is a dangerous way to live. I go to the pulpit as prepared as I can possibly get—but I still go with fear and trembling. What if God decides to let me preach in my own strength? Horror of horrors! Interestingly enough, the better I prepare, the more He anoints. The more He anoints, the more pleasure and less strain the preaching of the Word is for me.

In his book *An All Around Ministry*, which is a compilation of addresses to ministers delivered to an "Annual Conference of the Pastors' College," Charles Spurgeon wrote, "I love to preach in such a mood, not as though I was about to preach at all, but hoping that the Holy Spirit would speak through me."[2]

What a wonderful way to approach the pulpit—indeed, the entire ministry: God working through me!

The best way to stay fresh is to know yourself, your own strength and weaknesses. Know your own temperament and why you need to get away with Him. Then let Him flow through you.

Perhaps you know this, but it is the perfect reminder. The Jordan River flows through the Sea of Galilee. It gives out what it takes in. The result is a fresh body of water, full of life, and still as productive as it was in the days of the Bible.

So may I be fresh all the days of my ministerial life!

10
A REVIEW OF MY INCREDIBLE JOURNEY

I still feel amazed when I reflect on the events that have occurred in my life to bring me to my current place of ministry. On that last Sunday night in May 1949, I was only two weeks from graduating from East Nashville High School. Questions were racing through my mind: *"Now what? Where do I go from here? If I go to college, why am I going?"*

I had already filled out an application for admission to Asbury College in Wilmore, Kentucky. When I came to the question concerning my field of study, I left it blank.

But this night *God* filled in the blank!

I wish the call had been exciting or spectacular with blinding lights or something, but it wasn't. Some pastors get calls that seem to light up the sky. For me, the call was more like lighting a candle. But that candle still burns.

Four of us young men in our youth group at church grew up together. The other three had received glowing calls to the ministry, but for me? It was just like those old pick-up ball games in our neighborhood. Again I was the last one chosen, so I was not surprised with my somewhat less-than-spectacular "call."

On this night in May after the pastor preached and opened the altar, I felt compelled to pray. While I conversed with God, a simple, calm voice almost apologetically said, "Gene, I've taken the others. I might as well take you too!"

I can just hear your response: "That's it?"

Yes, that was it. There were no blinding lights, stars, or tears of joy. And there was no excitement, except for that of my praying mother, who had been asking God to use me. But you need to know that while the call was very simple, the journey has been incredible. Had I known what a wonderful privilege I was receiving, I would have begged God for the opportunity to preach. But, of course, I didn't know. The whole thing just kind of happened.

God chose me!

In John 15:16, Jesus said, "You did not choose me, but I chose you and appointed you to go and bear fruit—fruit that will last."

And on this night He was choosing me. He chose me for a journey that has been so exciting that most of the time I have had to hold on with both hands.

I think I can relate to the way Mary must have felt when the angel said in Luke 1:28, "Greetings, you who are highly favored! The Lord is with you."

I wonder if this young peasant girl did not respond, "Who, me? You must have the wrong person!"

In fact, when told that God was going to use her in a special way, Mary went into a state of shock.

"How can this be?" she asked.

The angel explained to her that God simply wanted to use her body for the birth of His Son. He would take all the responsibility.

So Mary responded, "I am the Lord's servant" (Luke 1:38).

And so began an experience for Mary that has made her the envy of multiplied millions. What an honor to be chosen of God to "mother" His only Son, Jesus!

As far as I know, I have never been the object of anyone's envy. But God gave me the high privilege of working with Him and being on His team. I, too, have found great joy in being the Lord's servant.

Looking back over these 40-plus years, I am convinced beyond any doubt that God has given me a journey well beyond anything I ever could have chosen for myself. I would not have had the audacity to draw blueprints for a life as exciting and rewarding as the one God has given me.

Along the way I have had the privilege to pastor varying sizes of churches. And I have faced such a variety of situations that have been so exciting that I can honestly say there has never been a dull moment.

Earlier I mentioned my first assignment, at Hohenwald, Tennessee. This was a church most ministers would be reluctant to pastor. Our "house of worship" was an unfinished basement equipped with homemade benches, a potbellied stove for heat, and a piano that wasn't even close to being in tune—but that didn't really matter, because we had no one to play it anyway. About three weeks into this journey I found a gentleman who was sight-impaired and could play the guitar and convinced him that he was needed to help with our music. Since neither of us could read music, he played while I led in our very limited repertoire of songs. Frankly, I don't care if I never hear the song "Come and Dine" again! But there were people attending for whom Jesus died, so I gave it my best. I probably learned more during that pastorate than did the people I pastored.

While pastoring the rural church in Mirabile, Missouri, during the period of my studies at Nazarene Theological Seminary in Kansas City, we loaded up our two babies every Sunday for that 65-mile trip into the country. At that time the church was 10 miles from the nearest paved road, so it was a tough trip—especially in the frigid ice and snow of winter. We spent the afternoons in someone's home and made the journey back to Kansas City late the same night. Hard? You bet! But I would not trade anything for the experience of pastoring those loving people. The lessons I learned there were priceless. I would do it again in a minute.

I won't take you back to every pastorate, but I must go back to Gainesville, Florida. For it was there that God and the 12 people who helped us plant a brand-new home mission church taught me the pure joy of being in His will. It is exciting to be fed literally from God's hands, to witness His moving on the hearts of the people to be His instruments as they supplied all of our needs "according to his riches in glory" (Phil. 4:19, KJV).

The journey took a wonderful turn for good at Princeton, Florida. The lessons God taught me in that wonderful church were very special. I learned very clearly that

- not everyone would love me and approve of my leadership
- God would have the final word in directing my life if I would only listen
- God's people love a faithful pastor and his family with an incredible love

I still wonder why those dear people put up with me for 10 years. They loved my family and me with a passion. I loved them, and together we lived and worshiped in the near-paradise of south Florida.

In 1971 this incredible journey led to Wichita, Kansas, and a great inner-city church. Frankly, I took this assignment with mixed emotions. I loved the balmy breezes of Florida. It can get bitterly cold in Kansas in the winter. And let it be clearly stated—the larger the church, the more opportunities there are for problems. The pressure of major budget commitments can cause restless nights. In my opinion, to seek the extra pressures and problems could be considered insane.

However, if God is in the move, He will enable His person to rise to the challenge. He has given wisdom, energy, and grace in abundance. I followed a successful pastor who had been there 23 years, and most people thought they needed an interim man—one they could "chew up and spit out," as several said. If I'm interim, I've certainly been here a long time! The call was clear. No, I never sought this assignment. For that matter, I didn't accept this pastorate until the Father made His will perfectly clear to me. But once I knew His will, I have never looked back or wondered if I did the right thing.

There is no substitute for being in the clearly revealed will of God.

So, after almost a quarter of a century of service here, I am still having the time of my life.

Pressures? Yes. Problems? You bet! But His grace and guidance have led me on this incredible journey. And I also believe He still has some memorable moments for me in the future.

This journey we are taking not only involves our assignment at the house of worship where we pastor but also involves our personal lives. And in my life God has given me blessings well beyond anything I ever could have planned.

I'm so thankful that, as a sophomore in college, I found Bettye, who shared my love for God and His kingdom. Bettye brought a new dimension to my life. She was softer, smarter, and more sensitive. She was an excellent Sunday School teacher and totally committed to Christ. When we needed an organist, her commitment to the Kingdom led her to learn to play that instrument. She covered for many mistakes I made along the way. As I've already said, upon her death in 1991 many people wondered what I would do without her.

I confess, it is scary to think of continuing the journey of faith when one's companion of 39 years is suddenly gone. When you realize, as I did, just how vital that person was, you begin to feel great pressure.

But the journey is a journey of faith. I had to face the issue of the message I had shared for 40 years:

God's grace is sufficient for every need in our lives.

I had hammered away about faith in God's unfailing love, wisdom, and guidance. So what would I do with my own message?—live by it!

And as I did, the Lord brought Joyce into my life and convinced me more than ever of the truth of Prov. 3:5-6: "Trust in the Lord with all your heart and lean not on your own understanding; in all your ways acknowledge him, and he will make your paths straight."

In looking back on our separate journeys, Joyce and I can clearly see how the Father did indeed direct our paths. It is amazing to witness His hands picking up the pieces of our lives and making them complete.

The journey of faith that God set before me has turned out to be so exciting and rewarding that if I could go back to that May night in 1949, I would still beg God to take me on His team. Had God told me then what He had in mind for my life, I would not have believed it. Yes, at times the journey has been through the "zoo." But I have to tell you, my friend—

I'm loving it!

.

Notes

Chapter 1

1. Charles R. Swindoll, *Living on the Ragged Edge* (Dallas: Word, Inc., 1989), 21.

2. Viktor Frankl, *Man's Search for Meaning* (New York: Washington Square Press, 1984), 12.

3. James Stewart, *Heralds of God* (New York: Charles Scribner's Sons, 1946), 54.

4. W. T. Purkiser, *Image of the Ministry* (Kansas City: Beacon Hill Press of Kansas City, 1969), 28.

5. Stewart, *Heralds of God*, 47.

6. Ron Mehl, *God Works the Night Shift* (Sisters, Oreg.: Multnomah Books, 1994), 143.

7. Tim Hansel, *Holy Sweat* (Waco, Texas: Word, 1987), 79.

8. Ibid., 75.

Chapter 3

1. From *Pastors at Risk*, 34, by H. B. London Jr. and Neil B. Wiseman, published by Victor Books, 1993, SP Publications, Inc., Wheaton, Ill.

Chapter 4

1. Jack Wilson, *But Thou, O Man of God* (Liberal, Kans.: Alpinglow Publishing, 1991), 89.

2. Ibid., 91.

3. Ralph Turnbull, *A Minister's Obstacles* (Westwood, N.J.: Fleming H. Revell, 1966), 41.

4. Ibid., 43.

5. London and Wiseman, *Pastors at Risk*, 128.

Chapter 5
1. David Jeremiah, *Acts of Love* (Gresham, Oreg.: Vision House Publishers, 1994), 65.

Chapter 9
1. London and Wiseman, *Pastors at Risk*, 41.
2. Charles Spurgeon, *An All Around Ministry* (London: Banner of Truth Trust, 1900), 183.